SOCIAL DESIGN

Metropolitan College of NY
Library - 7th Floor
60 West Street
New York, NY 10006

SOCIAL DESIGN

Participation and Empowerment

Edited by
Museum für Gestaltung Zürich
Angeli Sachs

Essays by
Claudia Banz, Michael Krohn, and Angeli Sachs

Lars Müller Publishers

20 Social Design—Past and Present
Angeli Sachs

Urban Space and Landscape

32 **Campo Libero (The Innocent House)**
Conceptual Devices / Antonio Scarponi

36 **Reinstating Small-Scale Neighborhoods in the Megacity**
Gehl Architects

44 **Foodmet Market Building**
ORG Permanent Modernity

48 **Granby Four Streets**
Assemble

Housing, Education, Work

58 **Kalkbreite Residential and Commercial Complex**
Genossenschaft Kalkbreite, Müller Sigrist Architekten

64 **Coop Campus, Die Gärtnerei**
raumlaborberlin, Schlesische27

70 **Community Library**
Robust Architecture Workshop / Milinda Pathiraja, Ganga Ratnayake

76 **Khayelitsha**
Urban-Think Tank, Ikhayalami, BT Section Site C Development Committee, City of Cape Town

82 **Lycée Schorge Secondary School**
Kéré Architecture

88 Design Without Walls
Claudia Banz

Production

98 Ateliers Chalamala
Sibylle Stoeckli Studios, Fondation HorizonSud

102 Flying8 Loom
Andreas Möller

106 Cucula – Refugees Company for Crafts and Design

Migration

112 Paper Emergency Shelters for UNHCR
Shigeru Ban

118 Refugee Olympic Team Flag
The Refugee Nation, Yara Said

122 Hic et Nunc
Zurich University of the Arts / Karin Seiler, Antonio Scarponi, Martin Bölsterli

126 *mag*das Hotel
Caritas of the Archdiocese of Vienna, AllesWirdGut Architekten, Daniel Büchel

130 Social Design in Education and Research
Michael Krohn

Networks

138 **Fairphone**

144 **M-Pesa**
Safaricom, Vodafone

148 **One Laptop per Child**

152 **Solarkiosk**
Graft / Lars Krückeberg, Wolfram Putz, Thomas Willemeit with Andreas Spiess

Environment

160 **Little Sun**
Olafur Eliasson, Frederik Ottesen

164 **Warka Tower**
Architecture and Vision / Arturo Vittori

170 **Safir Water Filter**
Zurich University of the Arts, Formpol AG, Eawag

174 **MoSan**
Mona Chirie Mijthab

178 **10,000 Gardens for Africa**
Slow Food Foundation for Biodiversity, Terra Madre

184 Authors
187 Bibliography
190 Image Credits
191 Acknowledgments

The overpass of the central business district in heavy smog, Beijing, China, 2015

Garbage-strewn water canal in the second largest slum in Africa, Kibera, southwest of Nairobi, Kenya, 2010

Zaatari refugee camp near the Jordanian city of Mafraq, some eight kilometers from the Jordanian-Syrian border, 2013

Rescuers look for survivors and victims at the site of the Rana Plaza building that collapsed the previous day, Savar, near Dhaka, 2013.

Electronic scrap at a junkyard, Hamburg, Germany, 2013

Harvesters on a soy plantation in
Morro Azul, Mato Grosso, Brazil, 2012

Lyonel Feininger, *Cathedral,* cover
of the Bauhaus manifesto and program,
April 1919

Social Design—Past and Present

Angeli Sachs

Social design—design for society and with society—is not a modern invention. And yet, it is of such great relevance today, because the global growth economy and its consequences for people and the environment are putting many societies at risk, or are even pushing them to the limits of their capacity to survive. Those who are not yet in this situation are justifiably concerned about the future. It is becoming increasingly clear that the imbalance of resources, means of production, education, and future prospects is a significant part of the problem. Thus, as in earlier times of crisis—in contrast to growing tendencies toward nationalism and isolationism—there is much discussion today about developing an open and cosmopolitan social culture, and redesigning social systems and working and living conditions in a way that bears in mind their implications for the world as a whole.

Architects, designers, craftspeople, and engineers have always played a decisive role in shaping such a social culture. Their visions for a better and more livable world have driven and continue to drive their own work and their sphere of influence, and have been a valuable reference for their successors. A few of these seminal figures will be introduced here.

The English designer, writer, publisher, and socialist activist William Morris holds a special place in this regard. The pioneer of the Arts and Crafts Movement, with his view that art and society are interconnected, left a lasting mark. He understood his work as an alternative to industrialization and its harmful effects on people and the environment, as had been described, for example, by Friedrich Engels in his 1845 essay *The Condition of the Working Class in England*. According to Morris, true art should be "made by the people, and for the people, as a happiness to the maker and the user."[1] Consequently, he himself became a craftsman, designer, and producer of wallpapers, textiles, glass, and furniture, who assumed responsibility for the entire design and production process in his collaborations with other designers. The main principles he applied to his work were beauty, quality, truth to materials, and durability. And he found inspiration in nature as an expression of vibrant growth as well as the craftsmanship of the Middle Ages and the preindustrial era. Morris's designs marked a stark contrast to the poor quality of the industrially manufactured products of his day and were greatly influential in the evolution of the decorative arts far beyond Great Britain. His ideal of a balanced society based on communal ownership, exchange, and development opportunities for all is described in his 1890 utopian novel *News from Nowhere.* Although he attempted to draw closer to his vision through a number of initiatives, his artisanal and social commitments harbor an irreconcilable contradiction: the painstakingly handcrafted products were affordable only to a wealthy circle of art enthusiasts and thus inaccessible to the parts of society he intended to reach.

In the German arts and crafts reform movement, the aesthetic principles of the English Arts and Crafts Movement were more readily accepted than the social consequences. This was true of the attitude toward design and the organization of work as well as the reception of the new direction by the growing bourgeois society: "The private citizen who in the counting-house took reality into account, required of the interior that it should maintain him in his illusions," described Walter Benjamin quite accurately, here in the French context.[2] Only after World War I—which can be considered the first fully industrialized war—did social utopias play an important, if temporary, role. One example is Bruno Taut's portfolio *Alpine*

The textile printing workshop at Merton Abbey, ca. 1890. From a brochure published for the 50th anniversary of Morris & Co., 1911

Architecture, published in 1919–20, in which, according to Matthias Schirren, Taut sought to oppose the incomprehensibility of World War I with a moral dimension in both the universe and in art. This is particularly clear in the third and central part of Taut's portfolio, on sheet 16, in which the later planning commissioner of the city of Magdeburg and builder of urban housing estates such as the Hufeisensiedlung ("Horseshoe Estate") in Berlin-Britz spoke directly to the "People of Europe!" and integrated the following "sermon" into the cruciform text format: "Preach: be peaceable! Preach: the social idea: 'You are all brothers, organize yourselves and you could all live well, all be well educated, and at peace!'"[3]

The woodcut by Lyonel Feininger that illustrates the 1919 manifesto and program of the Weimar State Bauhaus uses a similar image, a Cubist depiction of a Gothic "cathedral under a starry sky." At a time of fragmented modernity, this harking back to the Middle Ages (like John Ruskin and William Morris had), to the Gothic cathedral as a Gesamtkunstwerk and the medieval masons' lodges, coalesced with the idea of creating something "third, new." As Walter Gropius, the first director of the Bauhaus, stated in the closing sentence of the manifesto: "Let us strive for, conceive and create the new building of the future that will unite every discipline, architecture and sculpture and painting, and which will one day rise heavenwards from the million hands of craftsmen as a clear symbol of a new belief to come."[4] This vision would only last a few years, as the Bauhaus, located in Weimar until moving to Dessau in 1925, developed from an initial focus on individual artistic and crafts production to become one of the most important educational institutions for industrial design, exerting a lasting influence on international modernism. A landmark in this development was the B3 tubular steel chair designed by Marcel Breuer in 1925. When compared to his African Chair of 1921, it demonstrates just how far the Bauhaus had come in those few years. Design and production were again separated, in contrast to the masons' lodge utopias of the founding years. The Bauhaus thus took the plunge into industrialization, which had at first, as with Morris, been considered more of an antitype than an example to be followed. The dilemma once again arose that these designs were more likely to find their way into the living environment of the wealthy avant-garde than be affordable to the general public.

This development should be seen within the political, social, and economic context of the period between World War I and the

1930s, a time first of inflation in postwar Germany, then a subsequent upswing in the intervening years, and finally the Great Depression from the end of the 1920s. After Hannes Meyer succeeded Walter Gropius as director of the Bauhaus in 1928, "social responsibility" once again became the focus. In addition to plywood furniture and wallpaper designs, experimental residential architecture and housing construction became an important field of activity, and indeed one of the central tasks of the Weimar Republic after the currency stabilized in 1923.[5] However, the Bauhaus was put under increasing political pressure by the rise of National Socialism, which first led to Hannes Meyer being fired in 1930, and then—despite all attempts at depoliticization—to a move to Berlin in 1932 under its last director, Ludwig Mies van der Rohe, and finally to its closure in 1933.

During this period, in the second half of the 1920s, Frankfurt am Main evolved into a center for social architecture and design. Under the municipal planning director Ernst May, eight housing estates offering some 12,000 apartments were built between 1925 and 1930 under the Neues Frankfurt housing program. The "subsistence-level dwelling" was also the subject of the second CIAM Congress in Frankfurt in 1929. This concept was manifested in estates such as Frankfurt-Praunheim and Westhausen, where modest-sized apartments were equipped with standard "type furniture" and for which streamlined construction processes, including prefabrication, were used by municipal construction firms. In Praunheim, a row-house development was built where owners would take possession and then remodel and expand the single-family homes.[6]

Collaborating with Ernst May in Frankfurt's building department were architects and designers such as Leberecht Migge, who designed parks and gardens; Margarete Schütte-Lihotzky, who with her team developed the Frankfurt Kitchen; and Ferdinand Kramer, who, besides designing buildings for the Westhausen Estate (with Eugen Blanck), created elements for housing construction in the Department of "Standardization," as well as simple, modular "type furniture" that was manufactured in some cases "by out-of-work carpenters at the municipal unemployment office" by order of a charitable household goods concern, the Gemeinnützige Hausrat GmbH. The Neues Frankfurt housing developments and Kramer's furniture designs, along with the nature of their production, formed the most convincing synthesis in terms of social design at this time. For Gert Selle, they were "perhaps the most mature forms of a reconciliation between the human hand and machines, living labor and mass production, a social spirit in production and pure utility of use, ever produced by Weimar Republic design."[7]

A different domestic concept altogether was envisioned by the universalist R. Buckminster Fuller with his Dymaxion House, which he began designing in 1927. The name is a portmanteau of the words "dynamic," "maximum," and "tension." This was not a piece of private property on claimed land, but rather an inexpensive mobile living unit with a hexagonal floor plan and a tripodal supporting mast in the center, to be mass produced with a small ecological footprint for the time. Buckminster Fuller thus assumed a world in constant change, distancing himself from building as "a strategic act of colonizing the Earth" and "taking possession of land as a 'claim,' very much in the American tradition of a strategy for settling a place."[8] Describing his Dymaxion House, Fuller says, "Having once freed our minds of the customs and traditions that have bound us since the days of the earliest shelters, we can attack this dwelling problem just as we would attack the problem of building some other device or piece of machinery that had never before been made.... Such a house would of course be immediately available, erectable in a period measured by hours rather than by months.... A house of the size represented by the model illustrated could be had for about $3,000, and the application of the time-payment scheme would bring such a house within the reach of practically all mankind."[9] Only two prototypes of the Dymaxion House were built after World War II, and became known as Wichita Houses. No investors could be found for their mass production.

Ferdinand Kramer and Eugen Blanck, Westhausen housing development, Frankfurt am Main, 1929

Social Design—Past and Present

After postwar reconstruction and the resumption of economic prosperity, the next important milestone in the development of social design was the change in political perspectives that came about with the social movements of the 1960s. The first report of the Club of Rome, put together by Dennis Meadows in 1972, and the first oil crisis in 1973 demonstrated the "limits to growth" of industrialized society, and took a clear stance against a faith in unbridled progress with the resulting exploitation of humans and resources. In terms of design, Victor Papanek took up a significant and still influential position in his critical book *Design for the Real World: Human Ecology and Social Change* (1971).[10]

This attitude is consistent with Italian designer Enzo Mari's "Proposta per un'autoprogettazione" (Proposal for Self-Design) of 1974. The project, developed for an exhibition at the Galleria Milano, involved making a simple set of furniture out of rough wooden boards and nails. It was conceived as a critique of the economic pressure exerted by the consumer industry, coupled with a demand for participation by the consumer, who in the process of building their own surroundings could discover and come to understand the designer's intent, but also vary it. The final product would take on its significance through the didactic value of this process. "Autoprogettazione" was thus part of a contemporary social context marked by the desire for autonomy, dialogue, and participation, as expressed for example in the *Whole Earth Catalog* (1968–72) or in Ken Isaacs's *How to Build Your Own Living Structures* (1974). Mari hoped that this idea would continue to be compelling in the future, and he turned out to be right. There are countless designers today who study his ideas and respond with their own creations.[11]

Enzo Mari in his studio with models from his "Autoprogettazione" project, Milan, 1974

Another influential concept is Joseph Beuys's "social sculpture," part of his expanded definition of art, which was based on his examination of Rudolf Steiner's anthroposophy. Beuys's famous quote "Everyone is an artist" refers to creative processes in which all members of society can participate in order to bring about social change. An important work in this context is *7000 Oaks—City Forestation Instead of City Administration,* which Beuys developed for the Documenta 7 in Kassel in 1982. First, 7,000 basalt steles were laid out as a wedge-shaped triangle on the Friedrichsplatz, where Beuys also planted the first oak with its corresponding stele. A coordination office was set up on-site that also served as a nonprofit organization of the Free International University (FIU), which Beuys founded in 1973 before the Documenta 6. The tree and stone together cost 500 DM. The more trees were planted in the city of Kassel, the smaller the stone sculpture became. The landscaping artwork that changed the face of the city was completed in 1987, in time for Documenta 8.[12]

After the rather materialistic 1990s, the discourse on social design has intensified again in recent years. Beside numerous theoretical articles, symposiums, and networks,[13] there have been several highly notable exhibitions: *Design for the Other 90%* at the Cooper-Hewitt, Smithsonian Design Museum, in New York in 2007; the five exhibitions of the Utrecht Manifest: Biennial for Social Design between 2005 and 2013; and the 15th Architecture Biennale in Venice in 2016 entitled *Reporting from the Front* and curated by Alejandro Aravena. An increasingly transcultural and participatory perspective has evolved that marks a shift from social design "for" society to design "with" society.

Joseph Beuys, *7000 Oaks – City Forestation Instead of City Administration,* Documenta 7, Kassel 1982–1987. On March 16, 1982, Joseph Beuys planted the first tree.

Social Design—Past and Present

The contributions assembled here represent a selection of the vast panorama of the current field of activity in social design from a European pespective. The criteria by which they were chosen include the social and creative quality of the project, the transparency of the corresponding processes, the dialogue with and participation of the people involved in the project, their empowerment in the sense of building their own basic necessities, the transformation of social conditions, and the sustainability of the initiatives. Presented are international projects in the areas of urban space and landscape, housing, education, work, production, migration, networks, and environment. The designs range from new infrastructure and the reclaiming of cities by their inhabitants to educational opportunities for all; from DIY houses to initiatives for the integration of refugees; from the solar kiosk, an energy source that facilitates sustainable development opportunities for communities, to planting gardens in various countries in Africa.

1 William Morris, *The Art of the People* [address delivered before the Birmingham Society of Arts and School of Design, February 19, 1879], Chicago, 1902, p. 38; see also Nikolaus Pevsner, *Pioneers of Modern Design: From William Morris to Walter Gropius,* London, 1936; repr. Harmondsworth, 1960, p. 23.
2 Walter Benjamin, *The Arcades Project,* trans. Howard Eiland and Kevin McLaughlin, Cambridge, MA, 1999, p. 360.
3 Matthias Schirren, *Bruno Taut: Alpine Architecture; A Utopia,* Munich et al., 2004, pp. 21, 75.
4 Walter Gropius, "Manifesto and Programme of the Weimar State Bauhaus," 1919, at www.bauhaus100.de. See Gert Selle, *Geschichte des Design in Deutschland,* Frankfurt and New York, 2007, pp. 129–30. In his 1918 architecture program for the Arbeitsrat für Kunst (Workers' Council for Art), Bruno Taut had advocated similar principles. See Kenneth Frampton, *Modern Architecture: A Critical History,* London, 1980, p. 108.
5 See Frampton, *Modern Architecture,* pp. 119–21; and Selle, *Geschichte des Design,* p. 158. The construction of the experimental Dessau-Törten Housing Estate already began in 1926, led by Walter Gropius.
6 See Peter Körner and Philipp Sturm, "New Building in Frankfurt am Main and Iquique," in *Making Heimat: Germany, Arrival Country,* ed. Peter Cachola et al., German Pavilion at the 15th International Architecture Exhibition 2016 – La Biennale di Venezia, Ostfildern, 2016, pp. 160–65.
7 Selle, *Geschichte des Design,* p. 164, otherwise see pp. 160–66. See also Jean-Louis Cohen, *The Future of Architecture Since 1889,* London and New York, 2012, pp. 176–85. Europe's development following World War I is described in this essay based on a few important examples in Germany. Further important references include housing construction in "Red Vienna," such as the Karl-Marx-Hof (1925–30), and the housing cooperatives in Switzerland, such as the Neubühl Werkbund Estate (1930–32).
8 See Claude Lichtenstein and Joachim Krausse, "How to Make the World Work," in *Your Private Sky. R. Buckminster Fuller: The Art of Design Science,* ed. Lichtenstein and Krausse, Zurich, 2017, p. 12.
9 R. Buckminster Fuller, "Dymaxion House" (1929), in *Your Private Sky,* ed. Lichtenstein and Krausse 1999, pp. 135–37.
10 See also the essay by Claudia Banz, "Design Without Walls," in this volume, pp. 88–95.
11 See Enzo Mari, *autoprogettazione?,* Mantua, 2014, as well as the exhibition *Do It Yourself Design,* Museum für Gestaltung Zürich in collaboration with MAK Vienna, 2015.
12 See Fernando Groener and Rose-Marie Kandler, eds., *7000 Eichen – Joseph Beuys,* Cologne, 1999, pp. 11–12. See also *Wikipedia:* "Social sculpture" and "7000 Oaks."
13 Important examples include the DESIS Network (www.desisnetwork.org) founded by Ezio Manzini and Design with the Other 90%: Cumulus Johannesburg Conference 2014.

Urban Space
and Landscape

According to the United Nations, 55 percent of the world's population, or 4.1 billion people, live in cities today, and by 2050 this figure is expected to rise to 68 percent. The UN's *Revision of World Urbanization Prospects* currently rates the Tokyo metropolitan area with its 37 million inhabitants as the largest of thirty-three megacities with populations of over 10 million. By 2050, India, China, and Nigeria alone are expected to contribute 35 percent to global urban growth.

Sustainable urban as well as rural development must take social, economic, and ecological aspects into account. It must provide all population groups with secure access to infrastructure and social facilities. And it must give them the freedom to identify with and help shape their own environment.

Campo Libero (The Innocent House)
Conceptual Devices / Antonio Scarponi

Italy
2016

The Campo Libero (The Innocent House) was designed for the Italian organization Libera (Associazioni, nomi e numeri contro le mafie). Among other things, the NGO is working to reactivate land confiscated from the mafia in the south of Italy and to establish a legal economic system based on social justice and designed to create livelihoods. For example, autonomous and cooperative farms are being set up that respect the environment and the dignity of workers.

    Antonio Scarponi's mobile, self-sufficient, and reversible pavilion is a tool in this process. It is designed with fold-out elements so that its volumes can be extended and adapted to the respective function. The integrated scaffolding forms the structural frame, while also offering access to the roof and the option of building another story. The interior of the pavilion can be expanded on-site using simple means. One element therein is the Sedia Libera, which emphasizes the "right to sit." The Campo Libero looks out across the land and is intended as a platform and venue for negotiations with the goal of reclaiming the archaic lyricism of the southern countryside.

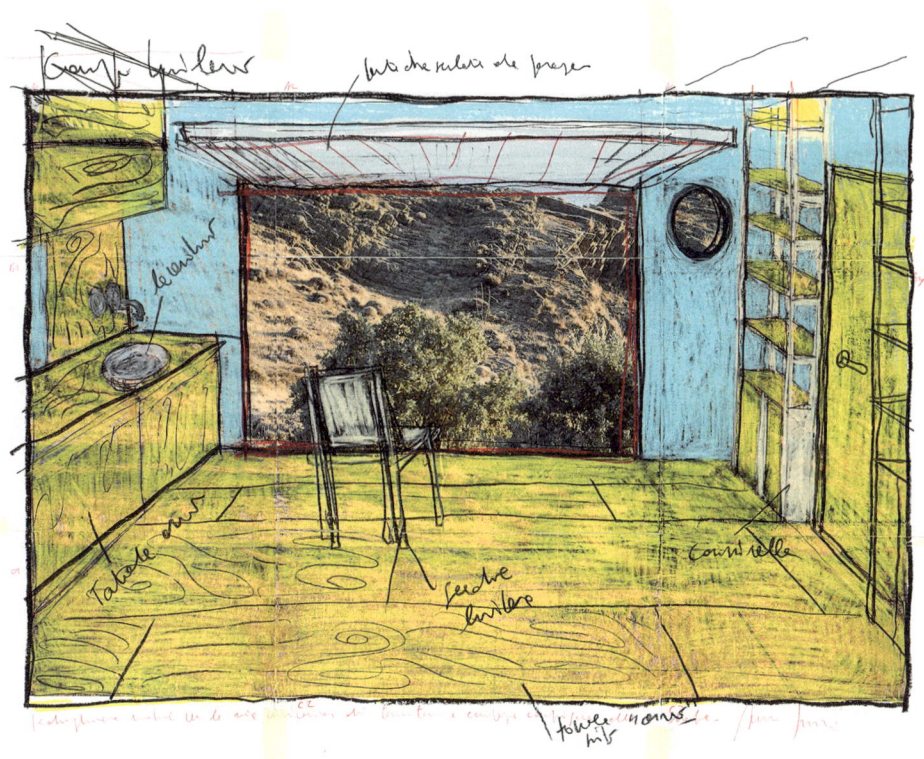

Sedia Libera is a chair designed specifically for the rural pavilion. It is part of a collection of furniture to be locally produced and nationally distributed involving the possibility of outsourcing manufacturing to refugees.

Urban Space and Landscape

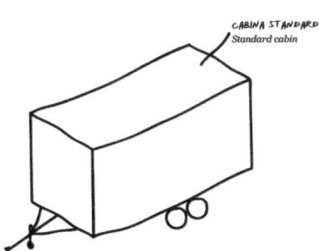

0. VOLUME INIZIALE "STANDARD" CONSEGNATO
Initial "standard" volume

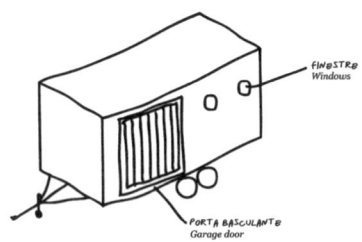

1. DETERMINAZIONE DELLE APERTURE SUL VOLUME INIZIALE
Determination of the openings layout in the initial volume.

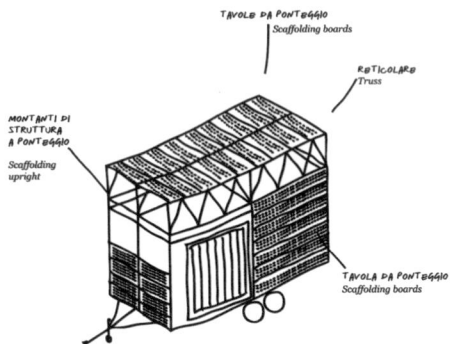

2. INTEGRAZIONE DELLA STRUTTURA A PONTEGGIO CHIUSA
Integration of the scaffolding structure (closed).

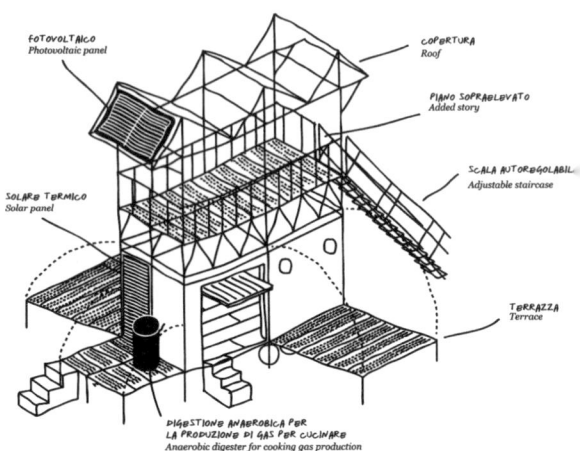

3. ESTENSIONE ED APERTURA DELLA STRUTTURA
Extension of the scaffolding structure (open).

The project was commissioned for the 15th Biennale di Architettura di Venezia, by *Taking Care,* the exhibition in the Italian Pavilion curated by TAM Associati. Five architects worked with five organizations to develop five mobile devices that activate Italian peripheries, promoting five common goods: health, legality, sports, education, and environment.

Urban Space and Landscape

Reinstating Small-Scale Neighborhoods in the Megacity
Gehl Architects

Chongqing, China
since 2008

Over the next thirty years, 300 million people will move to the cities of China. The focus of Gehl Architects, who collaborated with the Energy Foundation on their Sustainable Cities Program, is on how urban development, public space, and public transport link to environmental, economic, and social sustainability.

With rapid Chinese urbanization, the streets that have been the heart and the social, economic, and environmental backbone of the cities have been replaced with wide roads. The monolithic planning of China's new megacities, entirely designed for vehicles, has all too often razed existing human-scale neighborhoods that were once full of life.

The Chongqing project presented an alternative to this recent development and illustrated the qualities of the existing structure. The main goals were to extend and improve the existing micro network of interconnected streets and connect it to the newly implemented macro network of metros. The hope was to revitalize street life, improve the quality of urban public spaces, and preserve a sense of choice inherent in sustainable mobility.

The project illustrated how holistic thinking saves resources, focuses on people's lives, and can contribute to a sustainable and livable future.

Gehl Architects focus in their work on how the built environment connects to people's quality of life in urban spaces. By reducing the amount of land dedicated to highways and parking lots, they create more space for pedestrians, cyclists, and urban life.

Urban Space and Landscape

In order to improve the connection of pedestrian areas with the new metro line in Chongqing, Gehl Architects examined the existing urban structures and their use. This resulted in pilot projects for the design and networking of public spaces on a human scale.

Local planning and design teams implemented the pilot project for Pedestrian Route 3 in 2012. Taking measures such as simplifying orientation and reconfiguring intersections as well as expanding pedestrian areas to include leisure activities, seating, and lighting revitalizes the street as a space of social interaction.

Urban Space and Landscape

CHONGQING PUBLIC SPACE PLAN

The categories below organizes the streets of Chongqing, not just by scale and volume of cars as traditional, but by their quality as public space. It is not a description of specific projects, but a masterplan for how the streets should be develop in the future and what kind of qualities they should obtain.

A main public space network

The Public Space Plan
The aim of the public space network plan is to create a holistic vision for the public spaces of the Jiefangbei area, connecting all major destinations in a network of high quality for pedestrians, with a variety of spaces with different characteristics. Jiefangbei is a place for all in Chongqing, both locals and tourists, and should offer a world class environment of places, activities and destinations.

METRO PLAZAS
'Celebrate and invite people to use public transport by creating high quality metro squares as entrance plazas in the city'

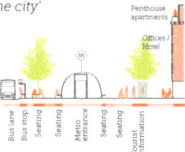

FORMAL PEDESTRIAN SPACES
'World class destinations for both citizens and visitors, connected in a high quality network for pedestrians'

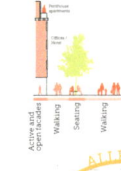

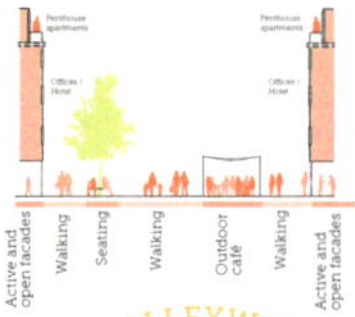

CITY STREETS
'Streets for all, offering an efficient & pleasant way of moving in the city by car, bus, bike or foot.'

SLOW STREETS
'A slow core in the city where the streets have public space qualities and invitations to stay. High priority for pedestrians, but access for all.'

ALLEYWAYS
'Human scale public spaces for urban recreation, offering an excellent environment for all senses'

PASSAGES BETWEEN UPPER & LOWER CITY
'Accessible & interesting connections between the different levels of the city where the passage becomes an attraction in itself'

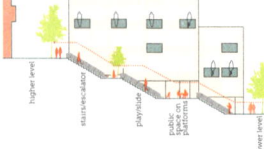

RIVERFRONT & PARKS
'A connected network of high quality green spaces, with plenty of opportunities to be active, and spaces to relax and enjoy the views'

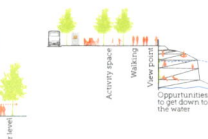

POCKET PLAZAS
'Pocket plazas offer a break from the city and can be busy or calm. They can also provide a small green space'

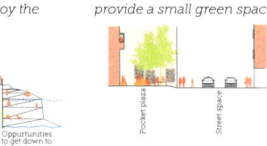

40

work for everyday | A fine grain network as oasises for recreation | A slow core with good connections to the water | A lively mixed use area for all of Chongqing | A connected waterfront for recreation & activities

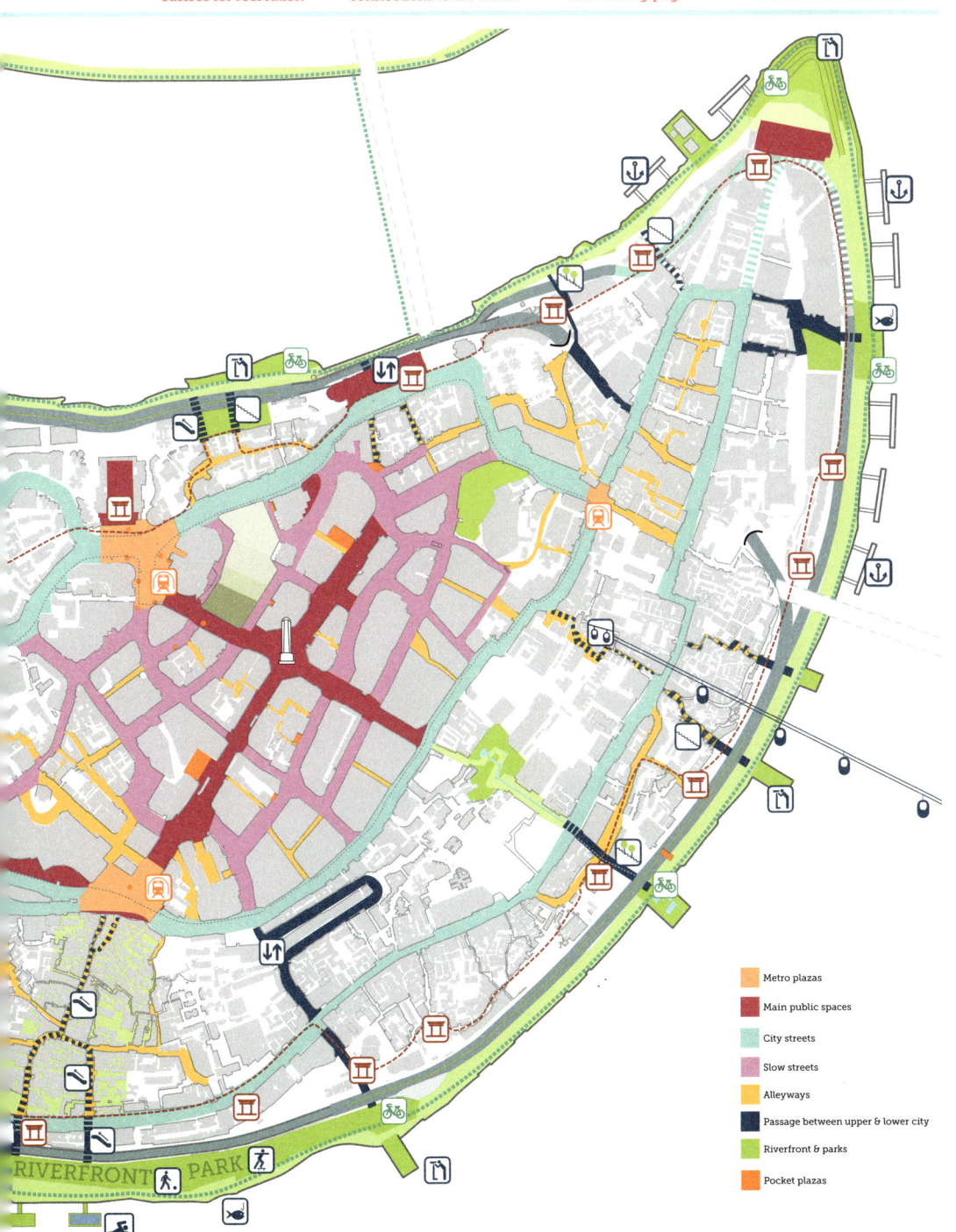

Legend:
- Metro plazas
- Main public spaces
- City streets
- Slow streets
- Alleyways
- Passage between upper & lower city
- Riverfront & parks
- Pocket plazas

Urban Space and Landscape

41

Previous pages: Following the successful implementation of the pilot project in 2012, Gehl Architects was invited to develop ten further pilot projects for downtown Chongqing. A visionary map was drawn up that classifies the cityscape into eight different street and plaza typologies, which in their interaction contribute to the quality of public space.

When cities are in the process of transformation, construction sites often disrupt public life. Instead of the usual perimeter fences, temporary two-story retail spaces were installed in Chongqing to activate street life and boost the economy.

42

Urban Space and Landscape

Foodmet Market Building
ORG Permanent Modernity

Brussels, Belgium
2009–2015

Brussels, the capital of Belgium and Europe, is dotted with monuments of the eighteenth, nineteenth, and twentieth centuries—nobility, bourgeoisie, and welfare state(s). Today, nearly 60 percent of Brussel's inhabitants are foreign-born. Inequality is at an all-time high. Brussels struggles to define a common space of shared aspirations, a space that is not dependent on the aspirations or hegemony of one single subgroup within the multitude. The battle of ORG Permanent Modernity has been searching—struggling—for a contribution to such a space, within the means of architecture and urbanism.

The Foodmet Market is located in an immigrant neighborhood only two and a half kilometers from Brussels Central Station. The market building, opened in 2015, is the first architectural step toward realizing the Meat Market District plan, which outlines the gradual conversion of an industrial slaughterhouse into a mixed-use urban environment.

The intention is to give form, pride, and civic presence to communities that have until now operated in an informal, semi-hidden world. In other words, define an architecture that is independently proud and generous, and yet serves beyond itself.

While guiding and designing the district redevelopment for more than eight years, ORG engaged the neighborhood to build consensus, created a "quality chamber" to review ongoing work, and developed a sequence of pilot projects where each investment triggered the opening up of a subsequent site, thus allowing for a domino effect of implementation.

Urban Space and Landscape

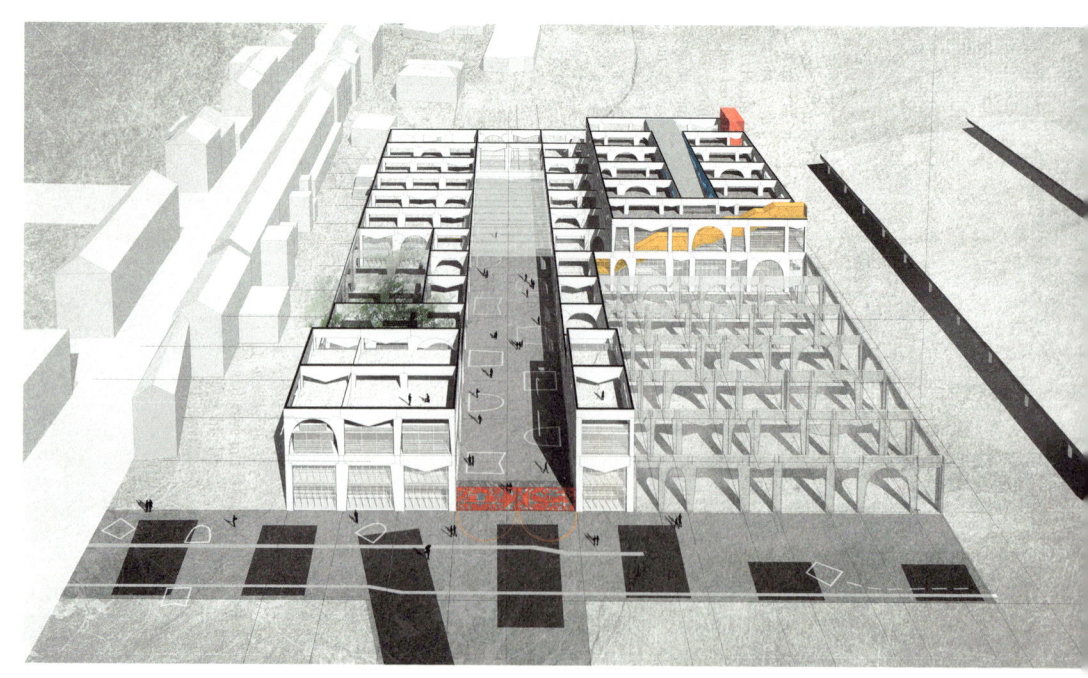

The platonic forms of the facade elements combine to create contemporary urban warehouses—buildings that have a clear urban form but no predefined content. The combination of these structures creates an environment with a civic presence.

The project includes industrial meat production facilities, various market stall types, logistics and parking spaces, and a large commercial roof farm with related retail programs.

Urban Space and Landscape

Granby Four Streets
Assemble

Liverpool, United Kingdom
since 2013

Granby Street was once a lively main thoroughfare at the center of Liverpool's most racially and ethnically diverse community. The demolition of all but four of Granby's streets of Victorian terraces during decades of "regeneration" initiatives saw a once-thriving community scattered. The resourceful, creative actions of a group of residents were fundamental to finally bringing these streets out of dereliction and back into use. After over two decades of work in order to reclaim their streets, in 2011 the residents entered into an innovative form of land ownership, the Granby Four Streets Community Land Trust (CLT), with the intention of bringing empty homes back into use as affordable housing.

    The multidisciplinary collective Assemble worked with the Granby Four Streets CLT and Steinbeck Studios to present a sustainable and incremental vision for the area that builds on the hard work already done by the local residents and translates it into the refurbishment of housing and public space as well as the provision of new work and enterprise opportunities.

Assemble refurbished ten derelict terrace houses on Cairns Street in Toxteth. The project was the result of a hard-won, twenty-year battle by local residents to save the houses from demolition.

Urban Space and Landscape

The approach is characterized by celebrating the value of the area's architectural and cultural heritage, supporting public involvement and partnership building, offering local training and employment opportunities, and nurturing the resourcefulness and DIY spirit that defines the four streets.

Urban Space and Landscape

Hallway

Living room

52

The design of the houses by Assemble uses simple, low-cost materials and includes a number of playful, handmade architectural elements that help re-establish the character of the homes following their long neglect.

Urban Space and Landscape

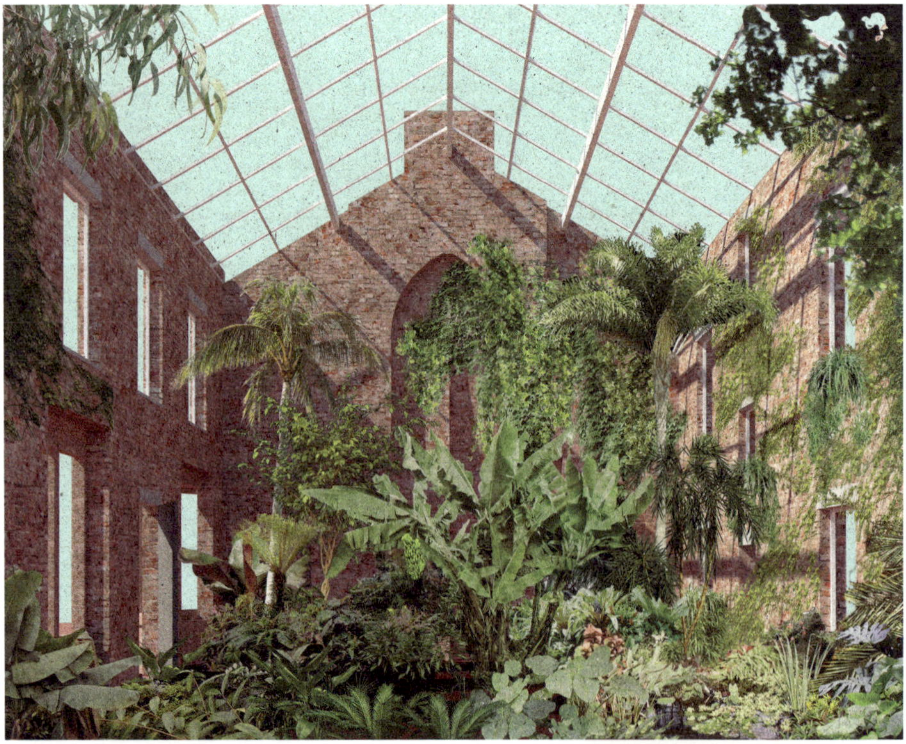

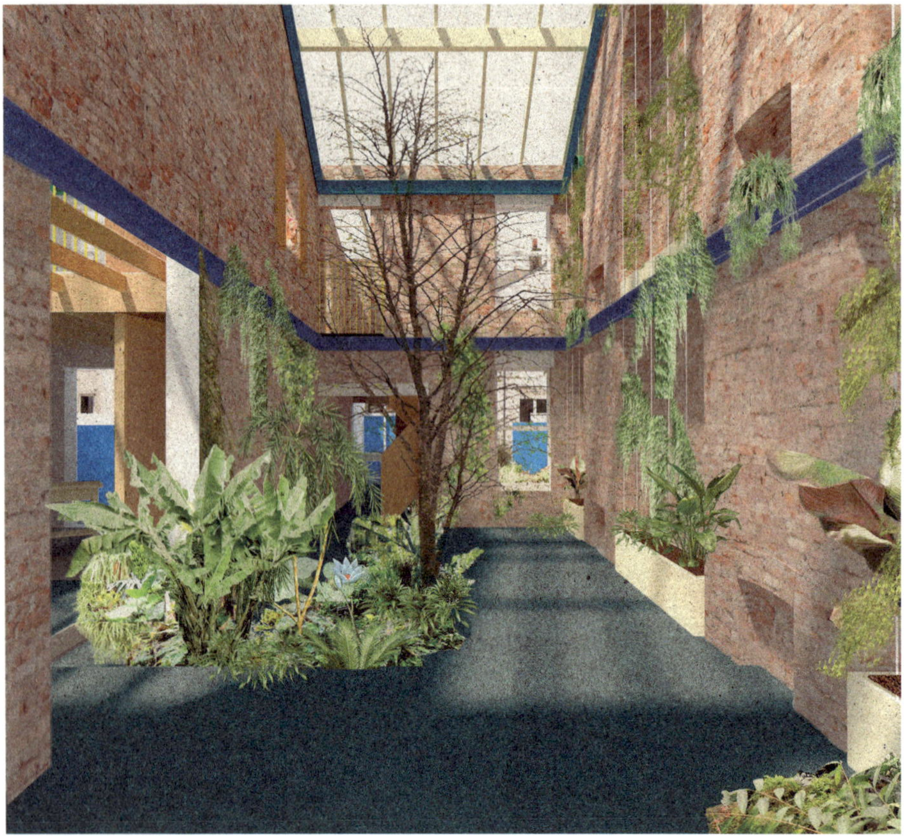

Left: Granby Winter Garden (2015, ongoing) will be a new community-owned space in the heart of the Granby neighborhood. Two Victorian terraced houses will be transformed into a unique resource for creative community action, cultural production, and exchange.

Granby Workshop is a manufacturer of architectural ceramics, launched by Assemble in 2015 as part of the Turner Prize. The first range of products were designed for the houses being renovated. The Workshop has since grown considerably, but the business remains strongly community orientated.

Urban Space and Landscape

Housing, Education, Work

The Universal Declaration of Human Rights (1948) states that every human being has the right as a member of society to social security and education, and the right to work under just and satisfactory conditions. The reality in many countries of the world is far removed from this ideal. The increasing imbalance in resources, the means of production, education, and future prospects is a global problem that threatens the international community.

To counteract this problem, social design relies on a new kind of networking between the individual, government, and the economy, using the tools of dialogue and participation. The key factor is always the emancipation of all those involved, combined with freedom, community, and justice.

Kalkbreite Residential and Commercial Complex
Genossenschaft Kalkbreite, Müller Sigrist Architekten

Zurich, Switzerland
2014

Since the nineteenth century, housing cooperatives have played an important role in Swiss housing policy. Swiss citizens voted in a referendum to increase the proportion of nonprofit housing in Zurich from one quarter to one third by 2050.

One of the most spectacular projects of recent years is the housing cooperative Genossenschaft Kalkbreite, which, in a participatory planning process, has created a perimeter block development above a tram depot operated by the Zurich public transportation company (VBZ), offering a wide range of spaces for living and working as well as commercial and cultural uses. This mixed-use environment, together with a broad social mix, fosters a high quality of urban life in the neighborhood. In addition to commercial and retail space, the complex has ninety-seven residential units accommodating approximately 250 residents. The wide range of apartment types, with one to seventeen rooms, offers options for different living arrangements and needs. To reduce the amount of space occupied by each individual, a number of common rooms are available for residential and commercial tenants. In its commitment to social, economic, and environmental sustainability, the cooperative is guided by the goals of the 2000-Watt Society.

The Kalkbreite building in its urban environment

Housing, Education, Work

Participatory planning and a mix of different living arrangements, common spaces, and areas for work and culture are key aspects of the cooperative project.

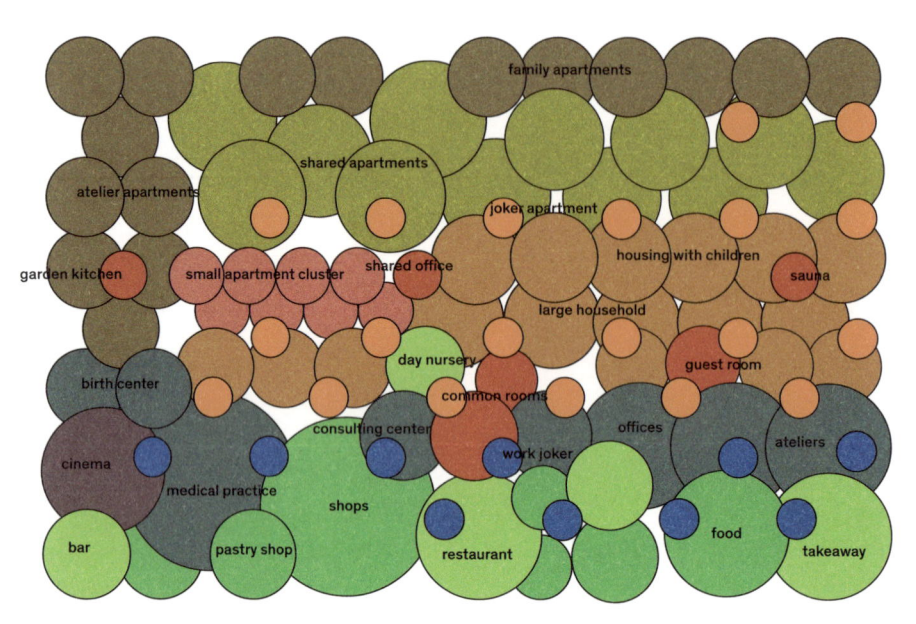

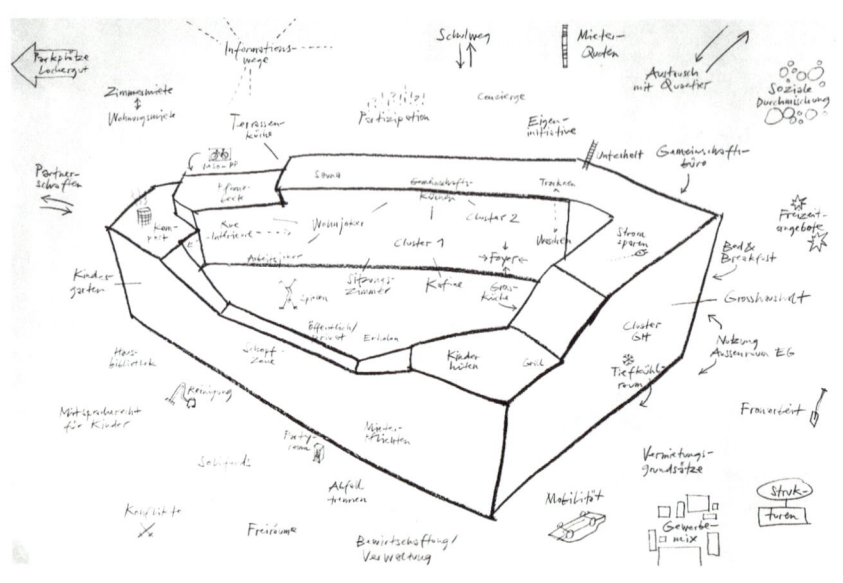

60

Stairway up to the courtyard and exterior
view from Kalkbreitestrasse

Housing, Education, Work

As with the common rooms inside the building, outdoor spaces are also shared, including a large green courtyard, sheds, and roof gardens.

The hall is the central entrance area and meeting place for residents, businesspeople, and also visitors staying at the guesthouse and using the conference rooms. The internal street, or Rue Intérieure, connects all six stairways with the entrance hall over several floors. A cafeteria equipped with a simple kitchen serves as a break room and shared living room for the residents of Kalkbreite.

Housing, Education, Work

Coop Campus, Die Gärtnerei
raumlaborberlin, Schlesische27

Berlin, Germany
since 2015

Like other countries, Germany has welcomed many refugees in recent years. In addition to government programs, various initiatives are contributing to the important task of their integration.

Die Gärtnerei (The Nursery) was established in 2015 as a follow-up to the Junipark experimental city art project in the fallow western area of the Jerusalem cemetery in Berlin-Neukölln. In a cooperative effort between Schlesische27 and raumlaborberlin, along with numerous neighborhood projects and volunteers, a garden has been planted and is being cultivated here with a team of refugees. In parallel, a vacant building was converted into a neighborhood meeting place and a school for everyday and practical knowledge as well as language classes. Programs such as the intercultural educational format Café Nana facilitate exchanges with the neighbors and other interested persons and groups.

Since 2017, Die Gärtnerei has been part of the Coop Campus project, which gives a growing network the opportunity to participate in the process of developing an open urban community.

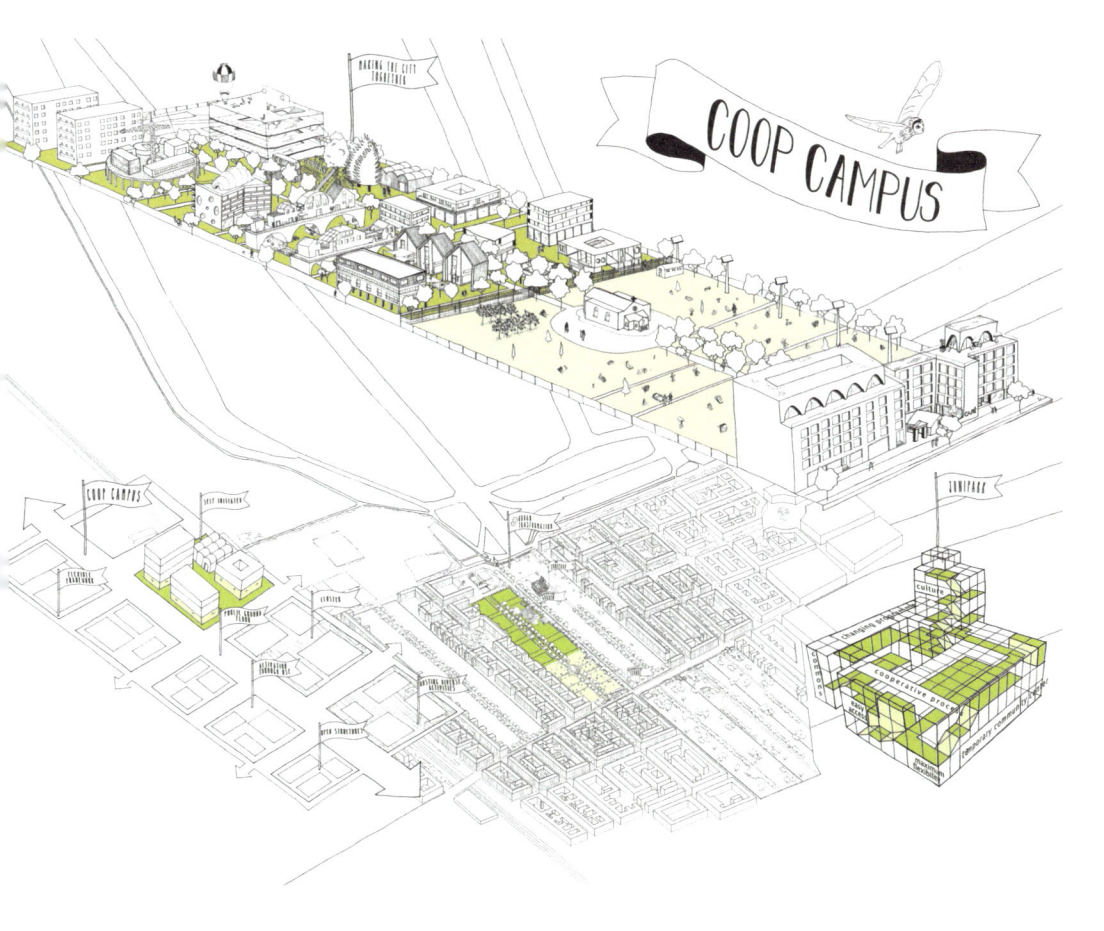

The Coop Campus is an ongoing development project on the site of a former cemetery. The catalyst was the temporary project Junipark, which was followed in 2015 by Die Gärtnerei. The Coop Campus then extended the concept by including urban design issues.

Housing, Education, Work

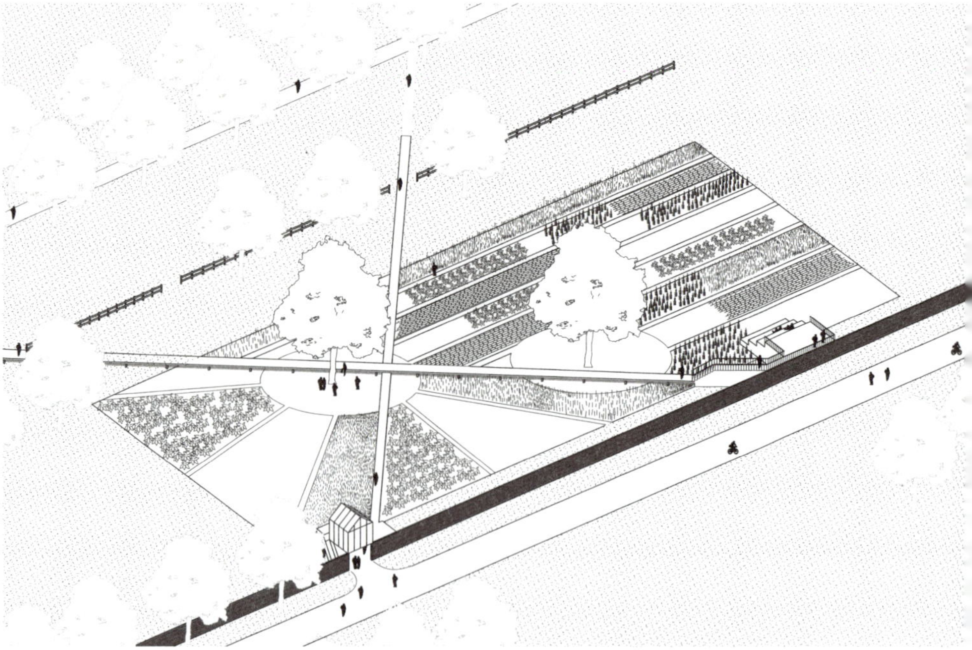

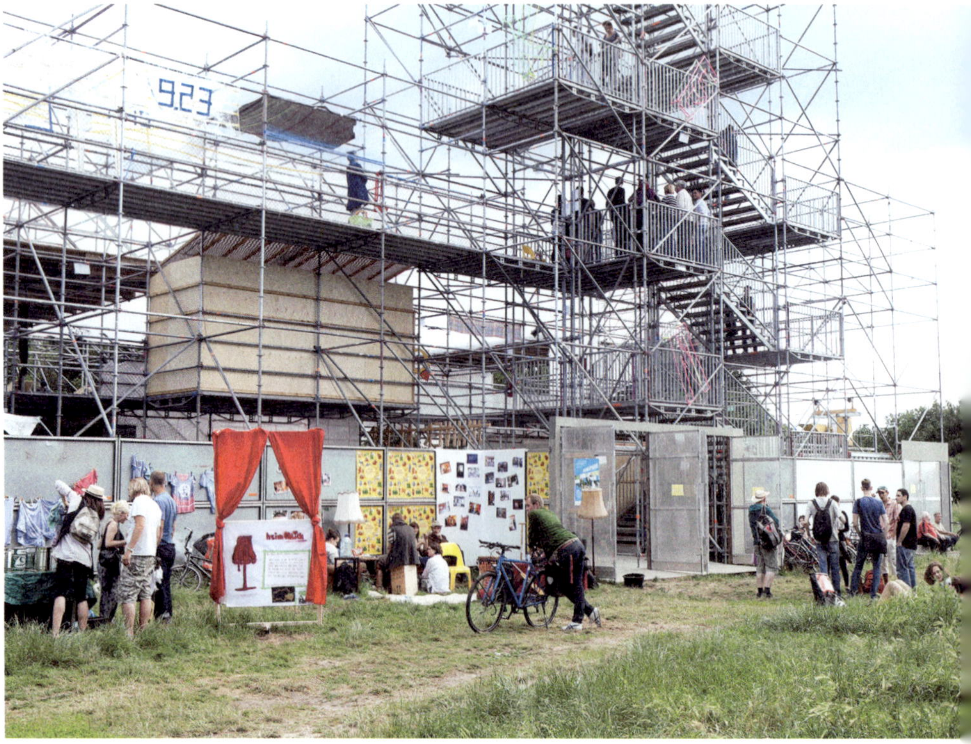
9.23

The Junipark urban art project was conceived as an open structure to be adopted for other uses (left page, below). The result was Die Gärtnerei, a project with refugees that includes two classrooms, a workshop, a kitchen, and a vegetable garden.

Housing, Education, Work

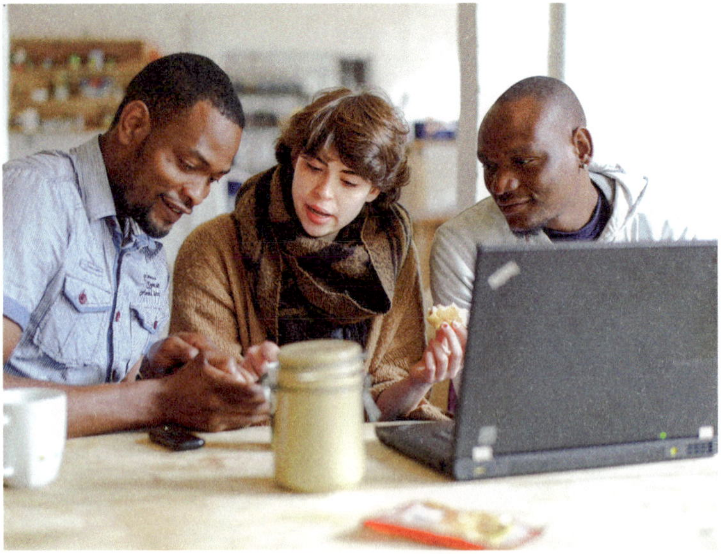

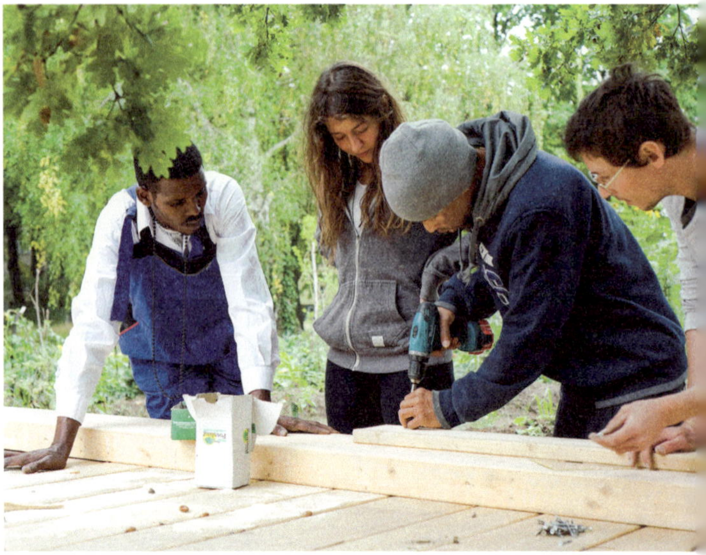

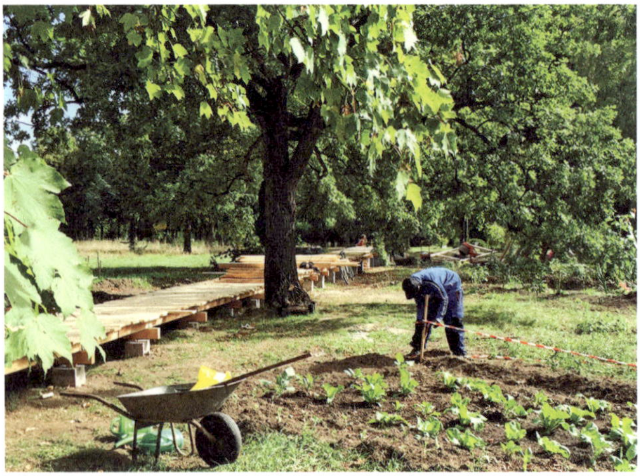

An old stonemason's workshop was later incorporated into the program at Die Gärtnerei. In addition to the garden workshop, a language school with volunteer teachers has been set up as well as other workshops, such as for woodworking, and also various cultural programs. At Café Nana, refugees tell interested guests about their culture and language at monthly get-togethers.

Community Library
Robust Architecture Workshop /
Milinda Pathiraja, Ganga Ratnayake

Ambepussa, Sri Lanka
2014–2015

For the developing parts of the world, a broader definition of the term "sustainability" is required, one that grapples with population increase, urbanization pressures, compartmentalization of knowledge and labor, post-disaster reconstruction, and a burning need to uplift the general social and cultural infrastructure.

This library project, built by soldiers with the assistance of the local community, focuses as much on the building process as on the building as physical artifact. Based on its vocational training strategies and environmental planning, the project attempts to heal social ruptures, build workforce capacity, disseminate knowledge, stimulate sustainable building, and strengthen social relations.

Programmatically, access to knowledge is reinforced as a weapon against ethnic disharmony and racial conflicts, and as a vehicle for proper economic development. The focus on knowledge creation and retraining—and the subsequent transformation of the army into a society-building institution—seeks to support the much-needed demilitarization of the country in the aftermath of its thirty-year civil war.

The library complex consists of three building blocks: the lending and reference section (main library), the children's library, and the research center.

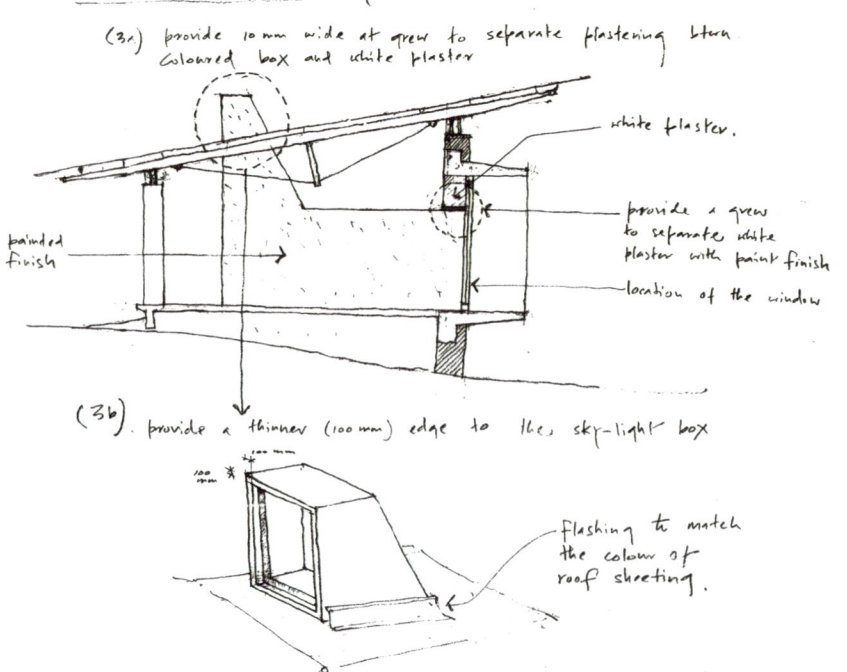

(3). internal brick wall.

(3a) provide 10mm wide at grew to separate plastering btwn coloured box and white plaster

- painted finish
- white plaster.
- provide a grew to separate white plaster with paint finish
- location of the window

(3b). provide a thinner (100mm) edge to the sky-light box

100mm

flashing to match the colour of roof sheeting.

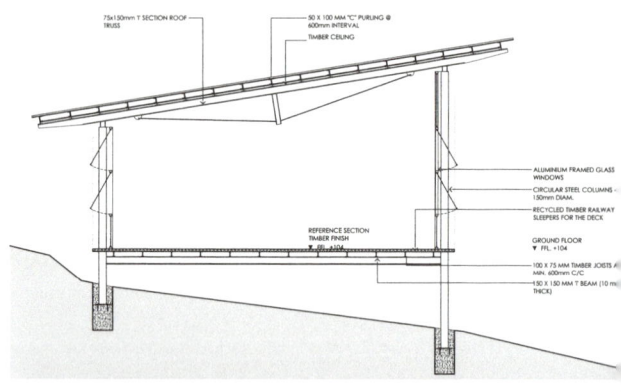

72

To accommodate the use of unskilled labor through targeted training interventions, buildings systems were designed to tolerate workmanship errors and forgive possible inaccuracies or shortcomings in manufacture, assembly, or use. The flexible, adaptable, and robust building solutions thus developed are proposed as a transferable building system to build similar community libraries across Sri Lanka.

LEGEND
1. ENTRY LOBBY
2. RECEPTION DESK
3. VIP AREA
4. KITCHENETTE
5. LENDING SECTION
6. COMMON LOBBY
7. OFFICE
8. REFERENCE SECTION
9. TOILETS
10. OUTDOOR DECK
11. COURT YARD
12. PAPER READING AREA
13. COMPUTER LAB
14. CHILDREN'S LIBRARY
15. RESEARCH AREA
16. CAFETERIA

Housing, Education, Work

73

The single-story building mass spans nonchalantly across the landscape, resting on soil through rammed-earth walls and floating on rocks through galvanized iron tubes. The library informally wraps around an internal courtyard, which is also an extension of the external landscape.

Housing, Education, Work

Khayelitsha
Urban-Think Tank, Ikhayalami, BT Section Site C
Development Committee, City of Cape Town

Cape Town, South Africa
since 2013

Shaped by apartheid-era planning, informal settlements in South Africa create poverty traps that restrict social mobility. The project moves beyond quick-fix development solutions that overlook the complexity of the problem by combining modular multistory building prototypes, inclusive spatial planning, and integrated livelihood programs that encompass microfinancing, renewable energy, urban water management, and skills training.

    The strategy redistributes existing floor plans to a two-story unit within a transparent urban readjustment methodology that synthesizes community preferences with urban planning frameworks. Recovered land is redesigned to free up public space for a coherent and safer urban environment, to install basic services, strengthen urban ecologies, and introduce additional sales and rental stock for cross-financing possibilities. Providing greater certainty about tenure by issuing accredited fit-for-purpose certificates, the scheme encourages incremental investment by residents to eventually reach building code compliance. This allows for a customized and flexible housing product for residents ordinarily shut out of the existing housing markets.

Community participation extends from
spatial planning to prototype construction
and evaluation.

Housing, Education, Work

77

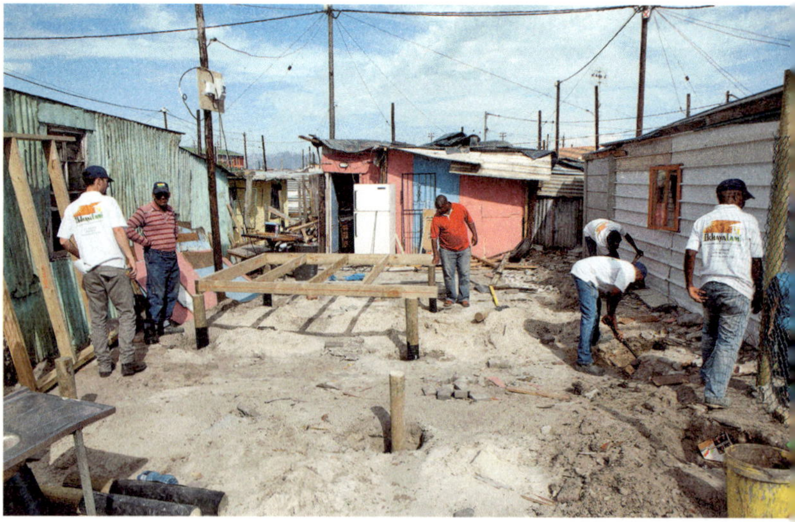

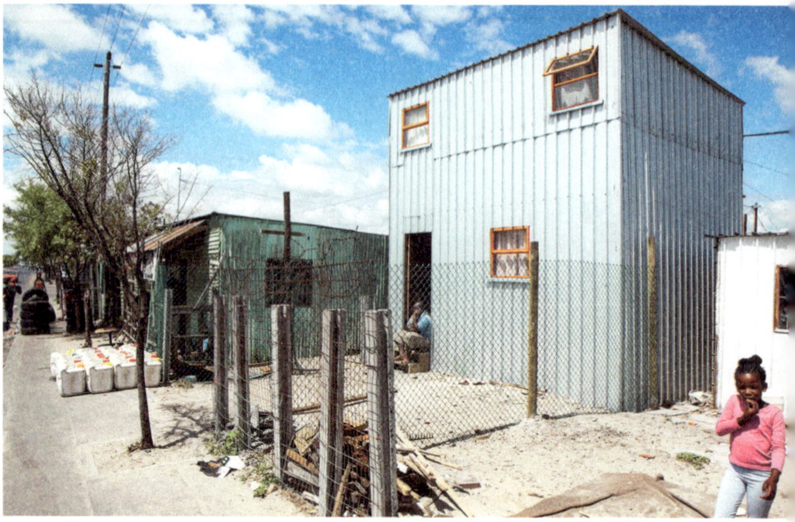

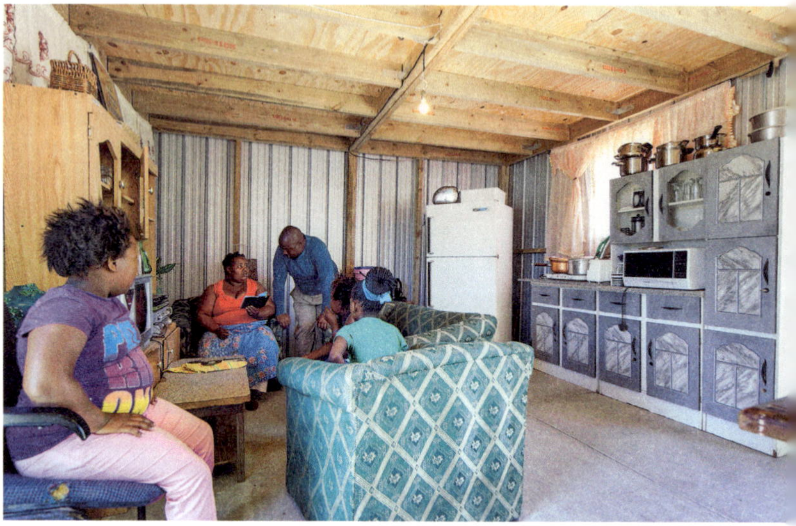

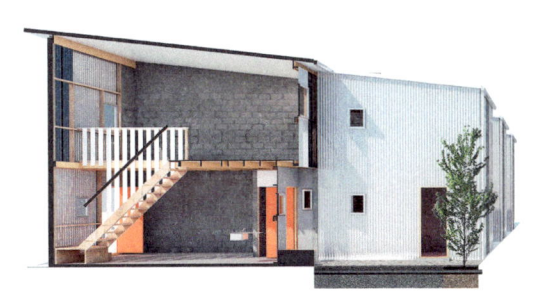

The project principles include the development of a scalable settlement upgrade methodology that offers immediate access to dignified shelter and basic services while establishing clear pathways to incremental formalization.

Housing, Education, Work

79

The housing unit upgrades are based on a core-and-shell principle in row-house configurations. The construction is based on local materials and industry practices and caters to six different unit sizes.

Housing, Education, Work

Lycée Schorge Secondary School
Kéré Architecture

Koudougou, Burkina Faso
2014–2016

Working across continents from Africa to Europe, Kéré Architecture strives to engage localities in their design and construction approach. Francis Kéré believes that architecture can be a vehicle for collective expression and empowerment, which is why his office works closely with local communities in all phases of design from planning to construction.

Located in the third most populated city in Burkina Faso, the Lycée Schorge Secondary School not only sets a new standard for educational excellence in the region but also provides a source of inspiration by showcasing locally sourced building materials in an innovative and modern way. The design for the school consists of nine modules that accommodate a series of classrooms, administration rooms, and a dental clinic.

The architecture not only functions as a marker in the landscape; it also demonstrates how creativity, teamwork, and local materials can be used to create a meaningful building with a profound and sustainable impact. Thanks to the success of the project, many residents have moved closer to the school and further educational projects have been developed in collaboration with Kéré Architecture.

Creating a sort of autonomous "village" condition, the radial layout of classroom modules wrap around a central public courtyard.

Housing, Education, Work

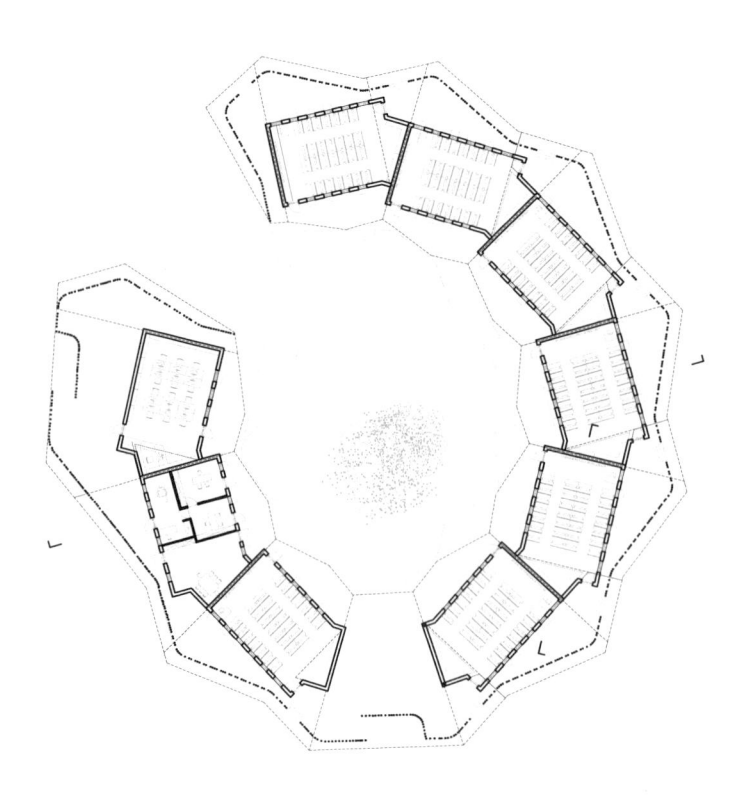

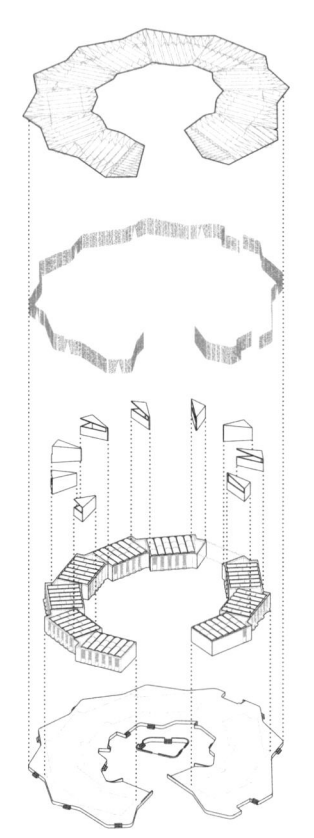

Metal Roof

Wood Screen

Wind Tunnels

Vaulted Classrooms

Concrete Platform

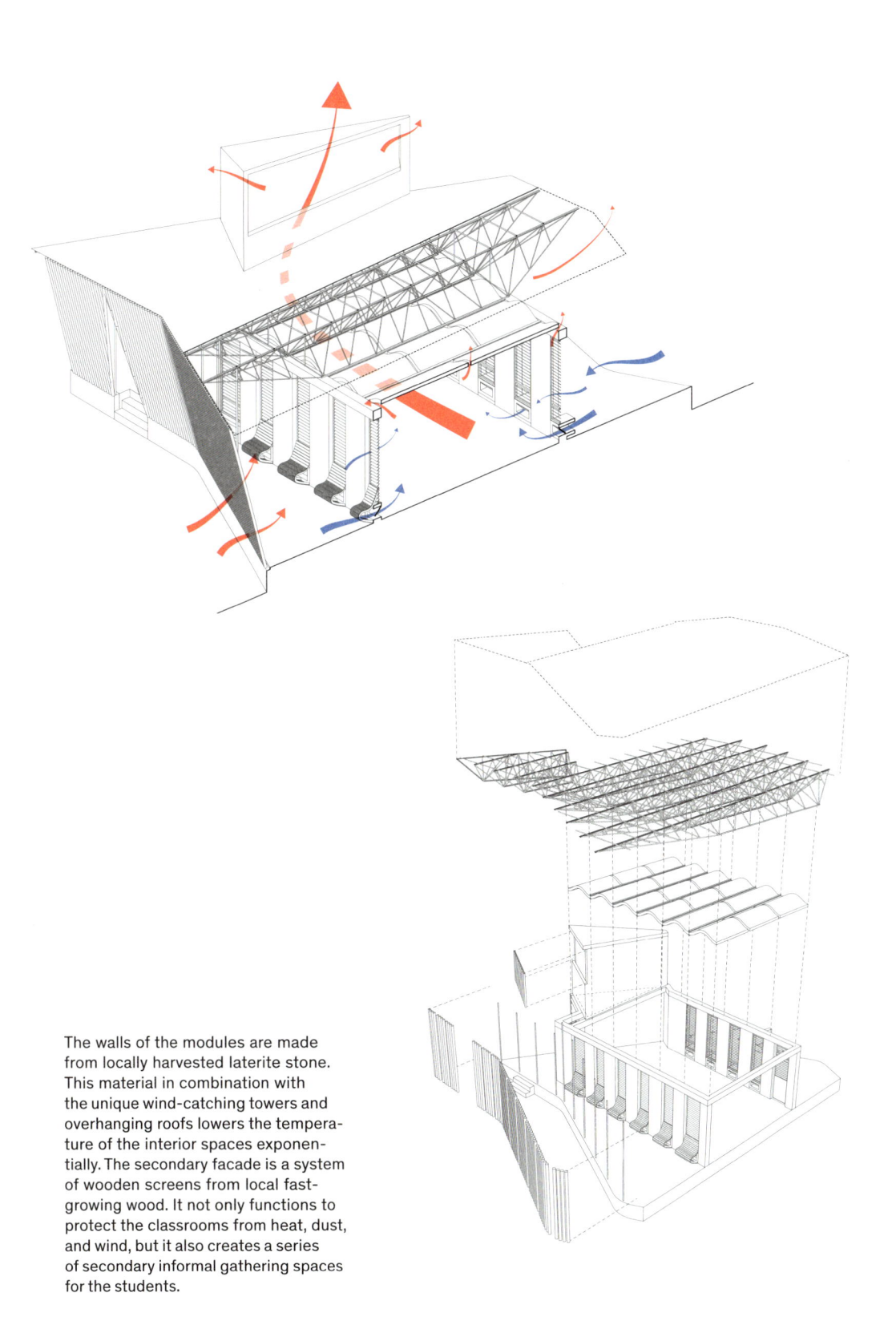

The walls of the modules are made from locally harvested laterite stone. This material in combination with the unique wind-catching towers and overhanging roofs lowers the temperature of the interior spaces exponentially. The secondary facade is a system of wooden screens from local fast-growing wood. It not only functions to protect the classrooms from heat, dust, and wind, but it also creates a series of secondary informal gathering spaces for the students.

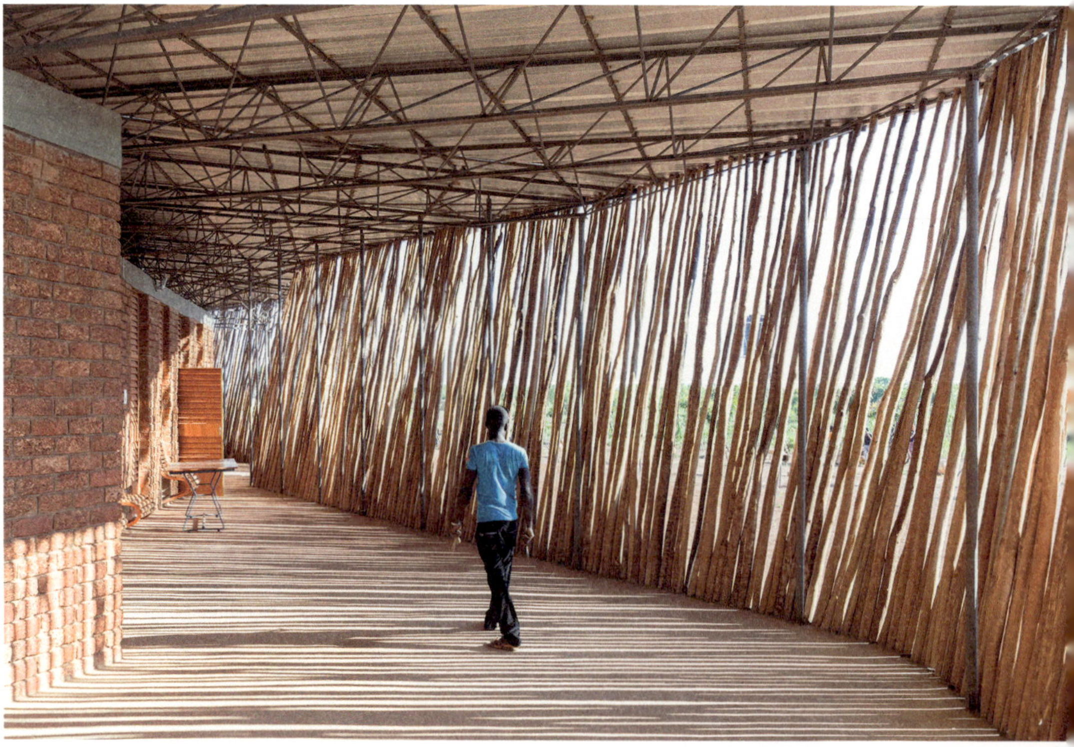

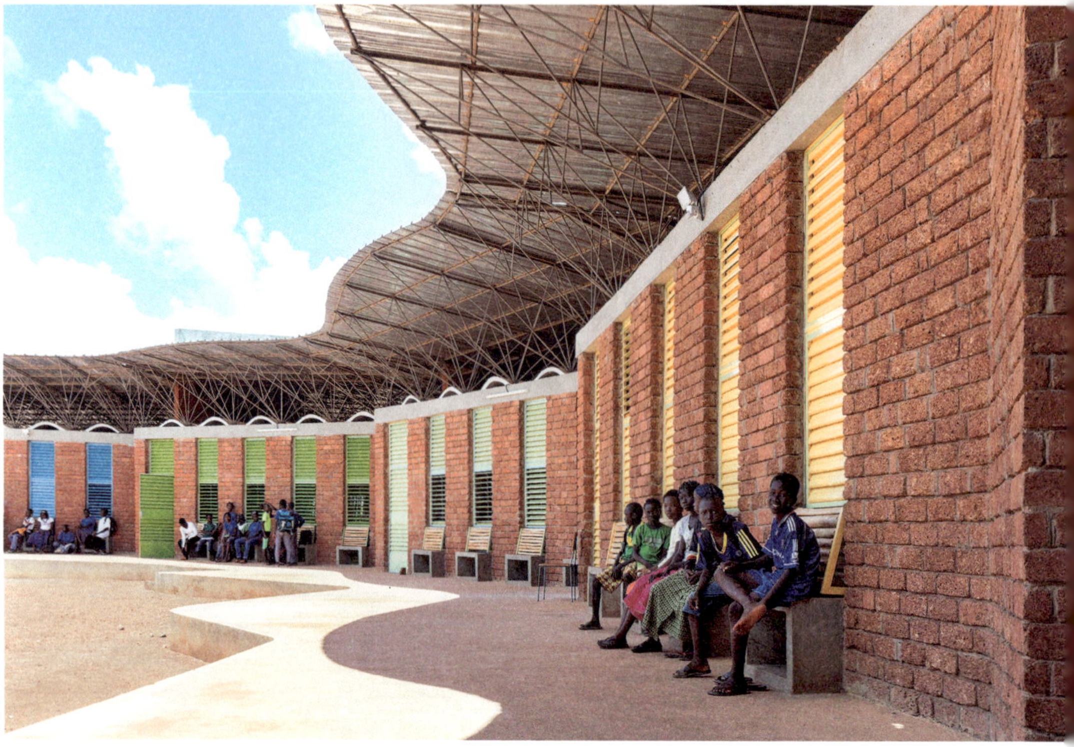

The school furniture is made from
local hardwoods and leftover elements
from the main building construction
such as steel scraps from the roof.

Housing, Education, Work

Design Without Walls

Claudia Banz

Wicked Problems

Education and action, knowledge and transformation, participation and responsibility, crisis and criticism: against the backdrop of these conflicting demands, the possibilities and limitations of design for the positive and socially conscious shaping of society and the environment have been pondered, argued, and negotiated intensely and not without controversy ever since the 1960s. Concepts like *plan-making, decision-making,* and *problem-solving* have been distilled as the core competencies that still today make up the heart of design thinking methods and social design toolkits. The way designers think makes the discipline more attractive than ever to policymakers and their representatives, who for their part are seeking solutions for the acute economic, ecological, and social crises of today. This creates a paradoxical situation: whereas non-designers implicitly attest to the discipline's high level of creative freedom and creative thinking, coupled with intuitive knowledge based on actual practice, and find it attractive for this very reason, the design discipline itself has been continually striving for the past fifty years to become more academic and scientific, with the goal of simultaneously improving design education. In the process, it has absorbed a number of elements from various management theories, computer technologies, and even from military strategies.

The concept of "wicked problems" was developed by Horst Rittel along with Melvin Webber in the 1969 essay "Dilemmas in a General Theory of Planning." Together they posited, "The search for scientific bases for confronting problems of social policy is bound to fail … They are 'wicked' problems, whereas science has developed to deal with 'tame' problems…. Moreover, in a pluralistic society there is nothing like the indisputable public good; there is no objective definition of equality; policies that respond to social problems cannot be meaningfully correct or false; and it makes no sense to talk about 'optimal' solutions to social problems ... Even worse, there are no 'solutions' in the sense of definitive and objective answers."[1]

This talk of wicked problems conveys a clear insight into, as well as an initial summary of, the discussions surrounding the question first posed in that decade: "Who plans the planning?"[2] Urban planning, architecture, and design were being put to the test at the time. The critique of the planner's role implied questioning his or her education and knowledge, and demanded an interdisciplinary focus. In the early 1960s, the so-called design method movement of Anglo-American origin was concerned with decision-making in the drafting process. It was a product of postwar optimism and the belief that scientific, rationally thought-out design could help make the world a better place. Lucius Burckhardt revealed this belief to be a "fundamental mistake ... Human environments are visible and subject to formal design to a limited extent only; they are comprised to a far greater extent of organizational and institutional factors. To alter these is a political challenge."[3]

Interestingly enough, in a parallel process, politics began to increasingly exploit social research for its own ends, which in turn adapted ideas from social engineering. Here, the maxim was that far-sighted planning policies that had not only economic factors but also social welfare and progress in mind needed a solid basis in evidence. Social indicators, social balances, and social trends have thus formed since the 1970s the cornerstones of an increasing interest in measuring society. It is hoped that through the collection of data sufficient knowledge can be gathered to effectively control and intervene in what is happening in society. Thus, we have long since been moving toward what Steffen Mau calls a "society of omnipresent *sociometry*."[4] He writes, "The cult of numbers, masked as rationalization, has far-reaching consequences: it also changes the way we construe and understand what is worthwhile or desirable. Indicators and metric forms of measurement each stand for specific concepts of social value not only with regard to what can be considered relevant but also what is or should be viewed as socially desirable and worthwhile."[5]

The Dilemma of Design

In the quantification of society, policymakers have found a seemingly good solution for wicked problems. The OECD Better Life Index and the UN's Sustainable Development Goals represent the enduring international belief and confidence, despite all setbacks, in the measurability of development, prosperity, and happiness on the basis of fixed indicators.

When it comes to problem-solving, the design discipline itself is caught up in a constant dilemma between the demands made on it and reality. Criticism of design education has continued in the same vein ever since the 1960s; Lucius Burckhardt, for example, pondered various aspects of design training in a number of essays. Toward the end of the 1990s, he came to the conclusion that the methods of teaching how to solve design problems were the actual problem and that the education of designers and planners was therefore in dire need of reform.[6] In her commentary on the 2011 symposium "Making/Crafting/Designing," polemically titled *Design leads us where exactly?*, Lucy Kimbell questions how future design practices might be developed and what kind of knowledge design students actually need: "I would say a passing knowledge of sociology and anthropology is essential now that design has realised it is profoundly social.... Ignoring the social worlds in which designed artefacts acquire their value and meaning is a weakness in much current design education."[7]

Designers increasingly view their own role as one of social innovators, as agents of social change, and are sought out as such by politics.[8] However, the processes and procedures by which public administrations or bureaucracies function can be complex. In the conference paper "Design for Social Innovation as a Form of Design Activism: An Action Format," the authors assert that design education has an obligation to support students in learning the theory and practice of a design strategy that rewards cooperation with and within public administration. "Further, education must equip them with the ability to navigate the internal machinery of government."[9] Perhaps designers will be able to guide political decision-makers toward an outside-in perspective. On the other hand, an inside-out perspective is also necessary. At the very point where these two converge, there is a lack of the holistic design education that various stakeholders are talking about and which would be necessary for a better understanding of the complex problems involved. In such contexts, the systemic drafting and planning methods described by Horst Rittel gain new currency. He had already warned about downplaying, oversimplifying, making false assumptions about, or idealizing problems; about unknown snags in thinking that are likelier to create new problems by incorrectly describing or delimiting the actual issue, compounding it into an unsolvable quagmire.

Consumption and Power

Design is a tool for producing social reality. It not only serves the purpose of promoting what is good and beautiful, however, but is also employed with negative intentions such as surveillance, oppression, or killing. Design is a reflection of certain power relationships and defines social hierarchies. It serves the neoliberal and digital revolution, the establishment of brands, and, with them, the enforcement of hegemonic Western structures and claims to power. According to Yana Milev, we have arrived "in the millennium of design power."[10] Essentially, this brings Victor Papanek's book *Design for the Real World* into the twenty-first century. In his book, published in the early 1970s, Papanek took a swing at his design colleagues and charged that they belonged to a dangerous group of professionals that were causing irrevocable damage to the Earth with their actions. Milev judges the strategies and real-world effects of current design ideologies using similarly dramatic rhetoric: "New ideologies such as *Green, Responsible, Safe, Sustainable* are merely new cover versions of design markets and design governance par excellence. In the new propagandistic guise of saving the world and in the name of creativity and sustainability, the design interfaces of governance have adapted themselves to the zeitgeist of cognitive capitalism."[11]

Today, clothing and food are key markets when it comes to ethical consumption. Fashion in particular is considered a "social trendsetter" and is therefore especially suitable for use as a political tool for government and development aid. Ethical fashion is meant to assist in implementing new business models that supposedly contribute to the empowerment of people, especially women, and help the poorest of the poor to gain a foothold in the global markets. With and through fashion, designers, startups, and labels can work actively against globalization and the associated concentration of power and lack of transparency. They advocate a new appreciation of local material and cultural, or rather artisanal, resources, for transparent and short production chains, new old forms of production and collaboration, as well as for sustainable products of higher quality and therefore with longer life spans. Fashion is capable of establishing an alternative political aesthetic that acts in the interests of fair wages and social justice, sustainable materials, zero waste, and closed-loop recycling; that takes a stand against climate change, against the environmental crisis, against exploitation, and mass consumption. In this way, fashion is capable of stimulating ethical, responsible consumption to a similar extent as food production. Despite all these quite positive developments, Elke Gaugele comes to a similar conclusion as Yana Milev, in that she sees design's potential to be used for resistance and activism at risk, since any and all criticism of the capitalist system is simply absorbed by osmosis by the ruling neoliberal elite: "Ethical Fashion with its value added chain of 'ethical capital' as a new sort of capital produces new fields of producing social and global hierarchies. Under the signs of a so called mutual benefit a new fashion value chain emerged fabricating a class of ethical people and morally superior consumers.... Currently these practices of a hierarchical structuring are redefined and adapted by the neoliberal global economy under the signs of ecology, social justice, and ethical consumption."[12]

Decolonization and New Knowledge

Victor Papanek is to this day counted among the few who also took the Southern Hemisphere into consideration in his design critique. In his aforementioned book, he emphasized the observation that the majority of designers work for the wealthiest 10 percent of the world's population. The remaining 90 percent would then fall through the cracks as potential beneficiaries of classic industrial design. Conversely, products made for mass consumption completely fail to meet the actual needs of this 90 percent. Fifty years have passed since Papanek made this claim. Even if a number of networks, initiatives, and projects are now developing approaches to a cooperative method of solving problems as equals with their users, they still cannot conceal the fact that the current ethical discourse fundamentally perpetuates the old forms of subjugation and the primacy of Western ideologies dressed in a new guise. The Indian scholar and women's rights activist Gayatri Chakravorty Spivak argues in her article "Righting Wrongs" that today's ethical discourse based on the idea of human rights "may carry within itself the agenda of a kind of Social Darwinism—the fittest must shoulder the burden of righting the wrong of the unfit."[13] The philosopher Achille Mbembe from Cameroon has developed the idea of "classrooms without walls" as an important pillar of decolonization. He accuses the schools and universities in African countries of Eurocentrism and calls for a radical break with traditional teaching methods and with the pedagogical dissemination of obsolete knowledge. In order to generate future knowledge, the classroom must be reinvented as a kind of platform on which the public audience meets in new forms of assembly; this could then lead, Mbembe maintains, to new forms of dissemination of different types of knowledge: "Decolonization is not about design, tinkering with the margins. It is about reshaping, turning human beings once again into craftsmen and craftswomen who, in reshaping matters and forms, need not to look at the pre-existing models and need not use them as paradigms."[14] This concept of decolonization is firmly directed against any sort of imitation or mimicry of European values. It even implies disregarding Europe. For intellectuals like Mbembe and others, Europe has outlived its usefulness as a model.

Mbembe attributes his realization that educational systems are the most important foundation for the ethical and moral revitalization of people and of social progress to Joseph Beuys. Although Beuys did not take dedicated action on behalf of decolonization, he did develop the most radical concept seen to date of an anthropological understanding of design; he saw human self-determination as the most elementary lever for shaping a more humane society. In 1972, Beuys presented his idea for a Free International School for Creativity and Interdisciplinary Research, which would make an individual's right to free development a requirement. Continuing this reasoning, he developed his revolutionary concept of art as "social sculpture," understood as a political productive force that "will only reach fruition when every living person becomes a creator, a sculptor, or architect of the social organism."[15]

Applied to design, this means that it can only truly be social and effective if it takes on the challenge of transforming itself into a "design without walls." Many grassroots movements grow up organically from the midst of society, such as the nutrition councils, the transition town movement, the degrowth movement, and the discussion surrounding "commons." There are concepts for so-called transformation design.[16] There have been and are currently many significant projects along these lines, several of which are presented in the exhibition *Social Design*. Nevertheless, designers must make much greater use of the potential and the potency of design in order to consolidate the ideas and visions of the aforementioned movements. In the interest of decolonization, design also has an obligation to do its part in dismantling existing international hierarchies and power structures. It must become transcultural and contribute to more creative self-determination in the comprehensive sense (social, economic, ecological). The basis for this once again lies in holistic education. Design universities and academies should therefore begin to take more seriously not only the possibility but also the responsibility to be proactive as pacesetters of change.

1   Horst W. J. Rittel and Melvin M. Webber, "Dilemmas in a General Theory of Planning," *Policy Sciences* 4, (1973), p. 155.
2   Lucius Burckhardt, "Who Plans the Planning?" (1974), in *Lucius Burckhardt Writings: Rethinking Man-made Environments,* ed. Jesko Fezer and Martin Schmitz, trans. Jill Denton, Vienna and New York, 2004, pp. 85–101.
3   Lucius Burckhardt introduced his response to the questionnaire sent to him by the International Design Center Berlin (IDZ) with the question of how our environment should be structured in order to earn the title of a humane environment. Lucius Burckhardt, "Design Implies Processes, Not Just Forms!," in *Design Is Invisible: Planning, Education, and Society,* ed. Silvan Blumenthal and Martin Schmitz, Basel, 2017, p. 55.
4   Steffen Mau, *Das metrische Wir. Über die Quantifizierung des Sozialen,* Berlin, 2017, p. 10.
5   Ibid., p. 14.
6   "Teaching people to deal with wicked problems is, in my opinion, the most pressing reform needed today in education in the fields of planning and design." Lucius Burckhardt, "Problem-oriented Project-based Teaching" (1999), in *Design Is Invisible. Planning, Education, Society,* Basel, 2017, p. 310.
7   Lucy Kimbell, "Making Crafting Designing, 2011," in *Design leads us where exactly?* (blog), March 4, 2011, http://designleadership.blogspot.com/2011/03/making-crafting-designing-2011.html; see also Lucy Kimbell, "Designing Future Practices," unpublished notes for a talk held at the symposium Making/Crafting/Designing, Akademie Schloss Solitude, Stuttgart, 2011. http://www.lucykimbell.com/stuff/KimbellMakingCrafting_Feb2011_public.pdf.
8   See Claudia Banz, "Zwischen Widerstand und Affirmation. Zur wachsenden Verzahnung von Design und Politik," in *Social Design. Gestalten für die Transformation der Gesellschaft,* ed. Claudia Banz, Bielefeld, 2016, pp. 20–21.
9   Davide Fassi, Anna Meroni and Giulia Simeone, "Design for Social Innovation as a Form of Design Activism: An Action Format" (2013), http://www.desisnetwork.org/2018/02/17/design-for-social-innovation-as-a-form-of-design-activism-an-action-format/
10   Yana Milev, *Designsoziologie. Der erweiterte Designbegriff im Entwurfsfeld der Politischen Theorie und Soziologie,* Frankfurt am Main, 2014, p. 729.
11   Ibid., p. 731.
12   Elke Gaugele, "On the Ethical Turn in Fashion: Policies of Governance and the Fashioning of Social Critique," in *Aesthetic Politics in Fashion,* ed. Elke Gaugele, Berlin and New York, 2014, p. 220.
13   Gayatri Chakravorty Spivak, "Righting Wrongs," *The South Atlantic Quarterly* 103, no. 2–3 (Spring/Summer 2004), p. 524, https://blogs.commons.georgetown.edu/engl-218-fall2010/files/Righting-Wrongs.pdf.
14   Achille Mbembe, "Decolonizing Knowledge and the Question of the Archive" (2015), https://wiser.wits.ac.za/system/files/Achille%20Mbembe%20-%20Decolonizing%20Knowledge%20and%20the%20Question%20of%20the%20Archive.pdf.
15   Joseph Beuys, "I Am Searching for Field Character" (1973), in *Art into Society, Society into Art: Seven German Artists,* ed. Caroline Tisdall, exh. cat. Institute of Contemporary Arts, London, 1974, p. 48.
16   See Bernd Sommer and Harald Welzer: *Transformationsdesign. Wege in eine zukunftsfähige Moderne,* Munich 2014. Welzer teaches transformation design at the Europa-Universität Flensburg; a transformation design study course was also introduced at the Braunschweig University of Art. Also worthy of mention here is the DESIS Network for Social Innovation and Sustainability, which was initiated in 2006, spearheaded by Ezio Manzini, and has since implemented numerous projects around the world as well as contributing to the progress of design research.

Production

The collapse of the Rana Plaza factory in Bangladesh in 2013, killing 1,138 people and injuring over 2,000, has become an appalling symbol of poor production conditions, exploitation, and inadequate job security—not only in the global textile industry but in many other sectors as well. But what does industrial production look like under the principles of social design?

Many of the projects presented here concentrate on helping people to build their own livelihoods. They not only try to lay the groundwork for a secure income for people who otherwise have no prospect of gainful employment but also enable them to work independently in their own social and cultural environment.

Ateliers Chalamala
Sibylle Stoeckli Studios, Fondation HorizonSud

Bulle, Switzerland
2012–2016

The collection of the Ateliers Chalamala is produced and packaged in the workshops of the HorizonSud Foundation in Bulle, Epagny, and Vaulruz by people suffering from schizophrenia. The sales room, the design of which was also part of the project, is located in Bulle, in the heart of the Swiss region of Gruyère, and the name "Chalamala" is a reference to the court jester of the Count of Gruyère.

    The designer Sibylle Stoeckli has reinterpreted a total of thirty wooden objects for everyday use in order to open up new, contemporary perspectives on the region's culinary products and to propose new ways of using these objects. The designs are characterized by a simple formal and symbolic language that plays with geometrical shapes and meanings. The objects are distinguished by their handcrafted quality and fair and regional production. The modularity of the forms and potential uses of these items symbolizes human values such as commitment, understanding, and openness.

The formal and symbolic language of the objects brings together circles and squares. Shingles and their typology are of particular importance in the collection, as they are also made up of circles and squares.

Metropolitan College of NY
Library - 7th Floor
60 West Street
New York, NY 10006

Production

The wooden objects in the collection have a whimsical air and entice people to eat together at the same table. Most of these utensils have multiple applications beyond their traditional use as dishes in the Gruyère region.

Production

Flying8 Loom
Andreas Möller

Hamburg, Germany
since 2009

With his Flying8 loom, Andreas Möller has revolutionized the craft of weaving and has facilitated the launching of companies in more than twenty countries on four continents.

He developed the complex yet easy-to-build and inexpensive handloom in 2009 during a weaving workshop in Ethiopia on behalf of the Deutsche Gesellschaft für Internationale Zusammenarbeit (GIZ, German Society for International Cooperation). Following the simple instructions and using standard tools, anyone can build the Flying8 in just a few days out of local timber, cardboard, cords, and adhesive tape. With the exception of the weaving comb, all necessary accessories can also be self-produced. Measuring 150 centimeters high and 120 centimeters deep, the loom is quiet, fast, and convenient. Möller left out some traditional weaving steps so that a weaver can quickly carry out the entire process from thread to fabric on his or her own.

Andreas Möller teaches building and weaving with the Flying8 loom in many countries, often as part of aid programs. Together with his former student Esmael Jemal, he runs the successful cooperation project "From the Hands of Ethiopia."

Training on the Flying8 loom in Ethiopia

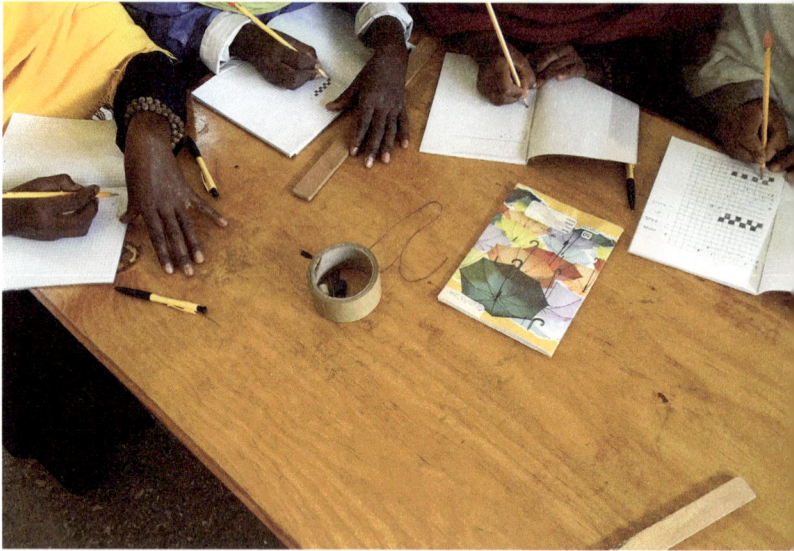

Esmael Jemal teaches a Flying8 weaving workshop in Addis Ababa, Ethiopia. A former student of Andreas Möller, Jemal is an ambitious young weaver who, together with four colleagues, runs a weaving mill using Flying8 looms.

The production of silk fabrics on Flying8 looms and training in how to build the loom in Meghalaya, India. The project to adapt local production to climate change in northeast India is being carried out in cooperation with GIZ and the company Seidentraum.

Production

Cucula – Refugees Company for Crafts and Design

Berlin, Germany
since 2014

Cucula sees itself as a creative space for experimentation, an experimental manufacturing operation, a laboratory for design and education, and a platform for intercultural exchange. Launched in 2014 at Kulturhaus S27 in Berlin-Kreuzberg, the project looks for new ways to educate and train young refugees. In the meantime, it has developed into an independent association and an established company that produces furniture according to the designs proposed in Enzo Mari's *Autoprogettazione* project. Collective creative production and related educational offerings provide international trainees with concrete prospects for finding a way into vocational training, even under difficult conditions.
     Some of the former trainees have formed the Cucula Council, a conceptual advisory board that helps to shape and advise the association's activities. Regular conferences are held as a way of breaking with the usual framework of the refugee debate. In addition to supporting immigrants in the Global North, Cucula increasingly focuses on the challenges and possibilities in the countries of origin.

In 1974, the Italian designer Enzo Mari published nineteen do-it-yourself furniture designs in his book *Autoprogettazione,* a milestone in design history. Forty years later, he gave the Cucula team the rights to use, recreate, and further develop his designs.

Production

Refugees Company for Craft and Design

EDUCATION   WORKSPACE   COMPANY

KOMPLICE CROWD

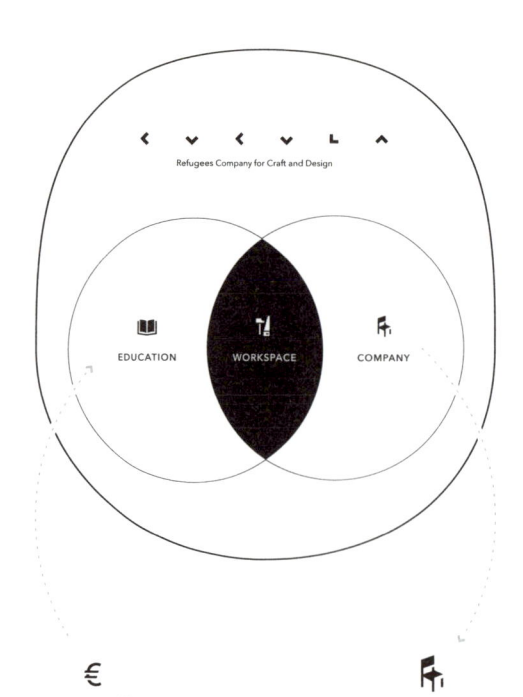

Enzo Mari's construction plans permit people with little experience in woodworking to produce high-quality, durable, and beautiful furniture with simple tools—irrespective of the language they speak.

The limited edition of the Ambassador Chair, an advanced version of Enzo Mari's Sedia Uno, was made of pine as well as timber stripped from refugee boats that had arrived in Lampedusa. The chairs tell the story of the Cucula trainees and invite people to sit, think, and listen.

Production

Migration

According to a report by the United Nations High Commissioner for Refugees (UNHCR), conflicts, persecution, and violence have led to record numbers of refugees worldwide—as many as 68.5 million in 2017. More than two-thirds of these people come from Syria, Afghanistan, South Sudan, Myanmar, and Somalia. Some 85 percent have sought refuge in countries close to home. So Europe is not impacted to the extent one may think. Nevertheless, there is an increasing trend toward nationalism and isolationism, which is reflected in the treatment of asylum-seekers and immigrants.

In cases where states do not support people in need, various initiatives seek to assist refugees and provide opportunities for integration in the country of arrival based on interpersonal exchange and empowerment.

Paper Emergency Shelters for UNHCR
Shigeru Ban

Byumba Refugee Camp, Rwanda
1999

Shigeru Ban has been making an essential contribution to humanitarian architecture since the 1990s as a part of his architectural oeuvre. Using unconventional, inexpensive, local, and sustainable materials and resources, he develops havens in conflict or disaster-affected locations around the world.

As a result of the racial friction that broke out in Rwanda in 1994, more than two million people have become refugees. The UNHCR initially supplied plastic sheets for emergency shelters, together with hatchets with which refugees could cut surrounding forests to make frames for the shelters. The resulting environmental devastation made it necessary to find alternative solutions. In response, the idea of using paper tubes as a low-cost component made of recycled material was introduced.

In the first phase of development, three shelter prototypes were built and tested for durability, cost, and termite-resistance. In the second phase, a pilot study explored the possibility of producing the paper tubes on-site. And in the third phase, fifty emergency shelters were built in Rwanda and monitored to evaluate the system in practical use.

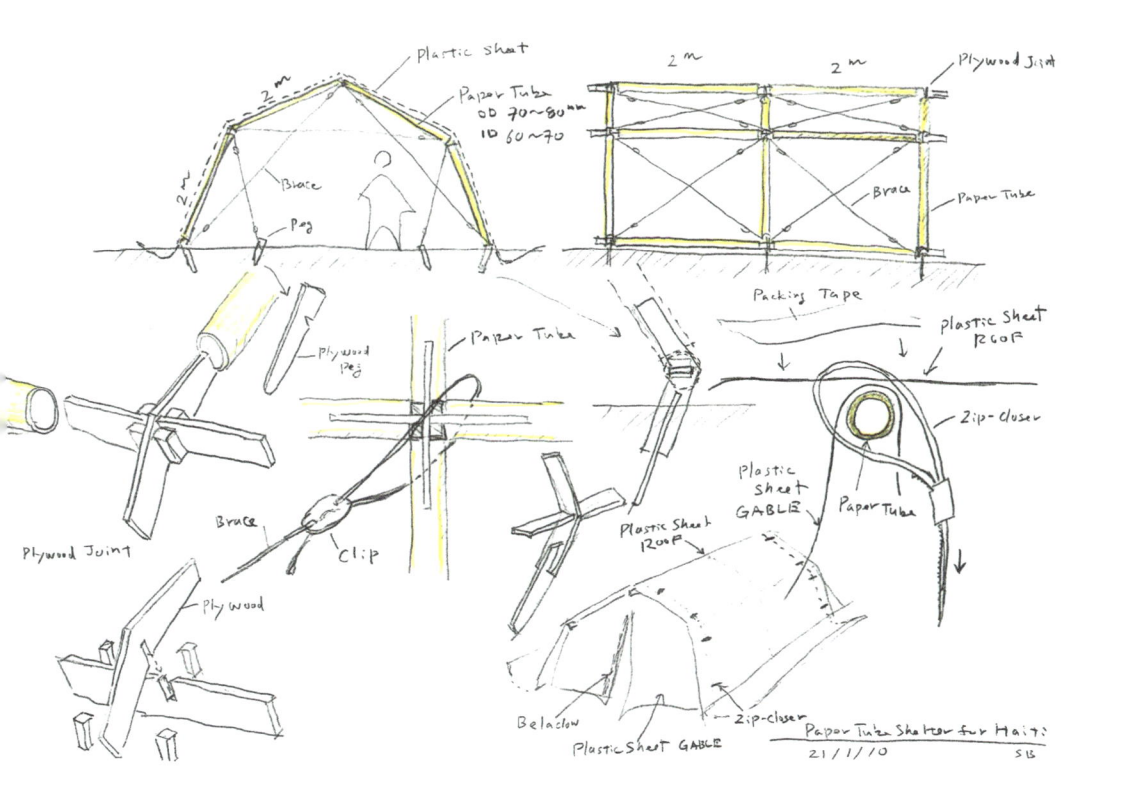

Sketch with structure, sizing, notes, connectors, tie-ins, and protective sheeting for the Paper Emergency Shelter for Haiti after the earthquake of 2010 that displaced 1.2 million people. Using and improving the construction he had developed for Rwanda and Sri Lanka, Shigeru Ban erected, together with an international project team, emergency shelters for refugees in Port-au-Prince, Haiti.

Migration

Volunteers build the frames for the Paper Emergency Shelter for UNHCR at Byumba Refugee Camp in Rwanda in February 1999. In total, fifty spacious and firmly anchored shelters were erected in the hilly terrain.

Migration

Annex D

The Components of The Paper Tube Refugee Shelter Kit

Components	Size	Quantity
Sheet A(Stripe reinforcements)	4m×6m	1
Sheet B(White, Blue)	4m×2m	2
Paper Tube A	Length 1,850mm	10
Paper Tube B	Length 1,300mm	12
Plastic joint		15
Plastic Anchor		6
Plastic Peg	Length 222mm	10(+1 extra)
Plastic Fastener	Length 300mm	29
Aluminium Stopper	Length 40mm	18
Rope	Length 3,500mm	18
Bag For Kit		1

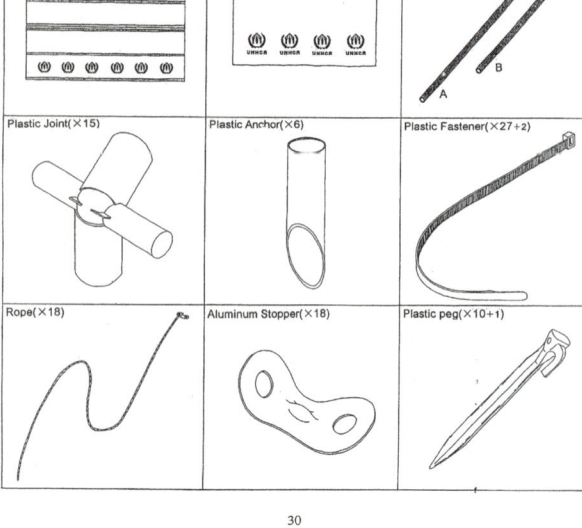

30

116

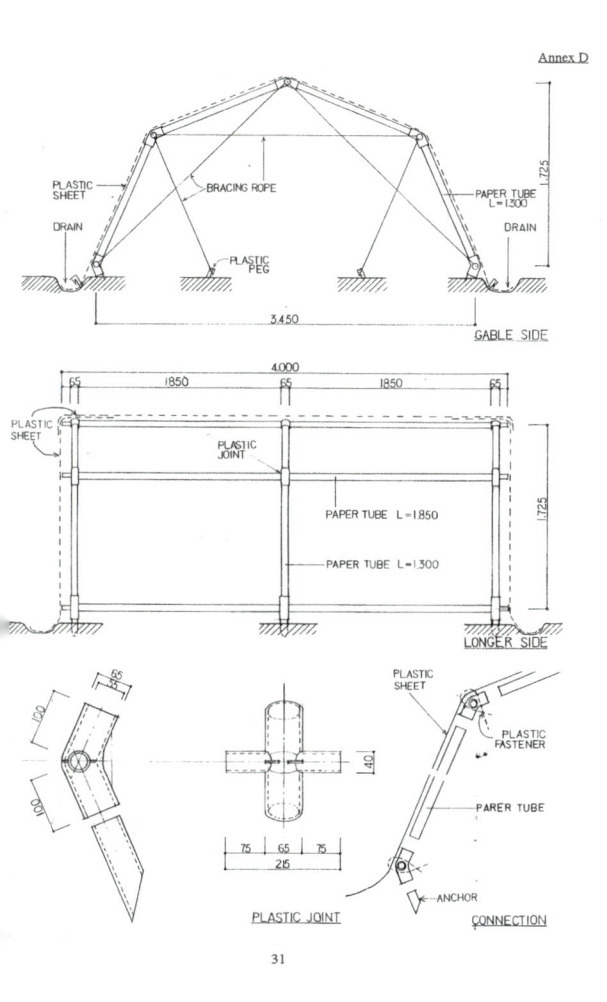

Building instructions with the components of the Paper Tube Refugee Shelter Kit and the construction of prototypes of Paper Emergency Shelters. These designs would be adapted during the Sri Lankan civil war in 2008 (bottom left) and for Haiti in 2010 (bottom right).

Migration

117

Refugee Olympic Team Flag
The Refugee Nation, Yara Said

Amsterdam, The Netherlands
2016

The Refugee Nation project is based on the idea of developing a symbol for the human rights of 65 million refugees worldwide.

At the 2016 Summer Olympics in Rio de Janeiro, a team of ten refugees took part in the games for the first time on the initiative of the International Olympic Committee. On behalf of the nonprofit organization The Refugee Nation and with the support of Amnesty International, the Syrian artist Yara Said designed the official flag for the team. The orange flag with a black stripe recalls the colors and design of the life jackets that many refugees wear when crossing the Mediterranean, which also forms part of Yara Said's own biography. An anthem was also composed for the games by Moutaz Arian, a Syrian composer forced to flee his country.

Refugees in Amsterdam now collaborate with the initiative Makers Unite to produce these flags from the remains of life jackets found on the Greek coast—thus earning an income. Beyond the Olympic Games, the flag and the anthem today symbolize the identity of and solidarity with those people.

At the opening ceremony of the Summer
Olympic Games in Rio de Janeiro 2016,
the first Refugee Olympic Team, composed
of refugees from several countries,
marched in the Parade of Nations in the
Maracanã Stadium under their own flag.

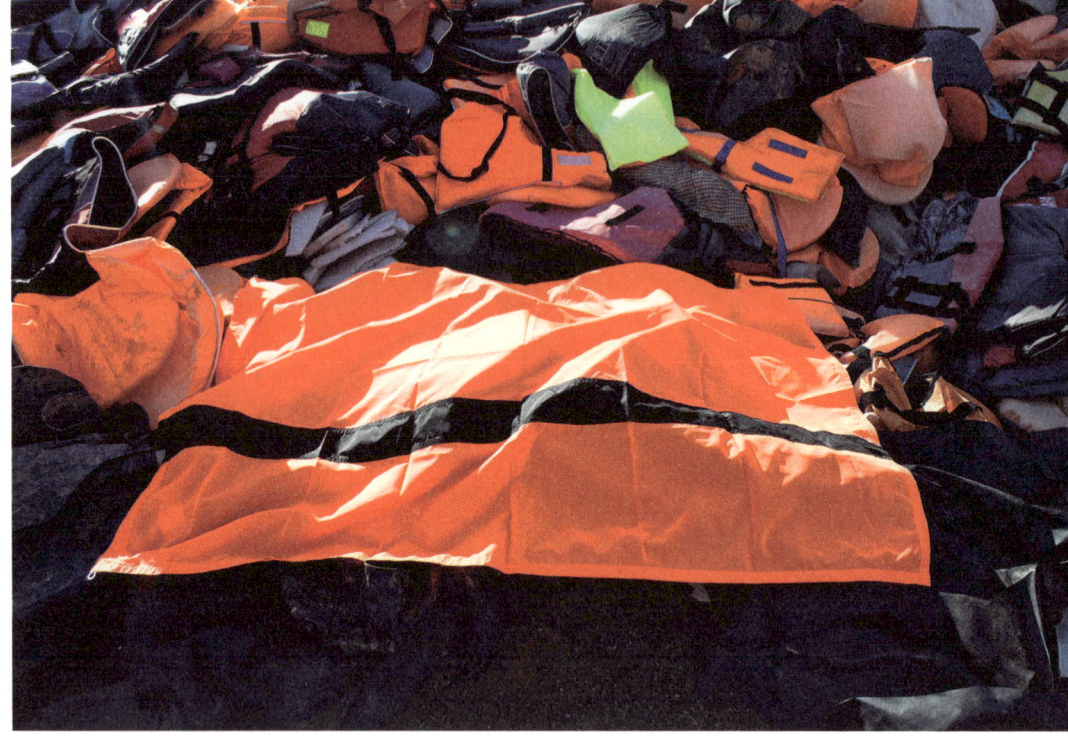

Yara Said, who designed the flag, says: "Black and orange is a symbol of solidarity with all these brave souls that had to wear life vests to cross the sea to look for safety in a new country. Since I had to wear one, I have a personal engagement with these life vests, and these two colors."

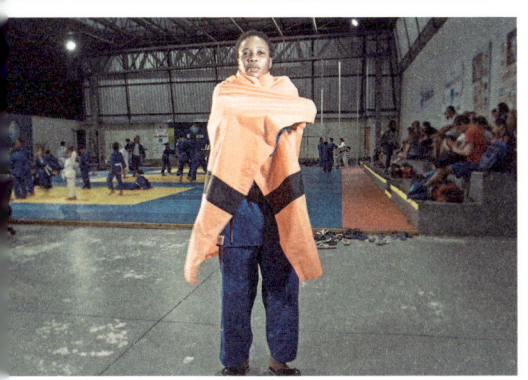

Migration

Hic et Nunc
Zurich University of the Arts /
Karin Seiler, Antonio Scarponi, Martin Bölsterli

Zurich, Switzerland
since 2016

Hic et Nunc (Here and Now) asks what design can do in emergency situations in a short amount of time and with limited resources. Developed at Zurich University of the Arts in collaboration with the Zurich-based professional organization AOZ, the interdisciplinary teaching formats developed by Hic et Nunc offer bachelor students the opportunity to engage with the diverse challenges of migration and to experience and critically reflect on the direct effects of their actions as designers.

Around 250 asylum seekers from Eritrea, Syria, Afghanistan, and Iraq have been living in temporary housing set up in Hall 9 at the trade fair grounds in Zurich-Oerlikon since January 2016. Container-like housing units are each shared by four people. The close cooperation with the operator AOZ puts the students in contact with these people and facilitates their participation in projects aimed at improving the living conditions of the refugees and employees in the exhibition hall. For example, benches have been built that also serve as charging stations for mobile phones, along with modular shelving, a simple gym, a women's space, and the prototype for a veranda that adds an additional, semi-private space to the housing units.

The library, which consists of a cleverly designed wall of books and a reading corner, defines a previously unused part of Hall 9 as a place of concentration. More than 300 books were collected during a "bookraising" event at Zurich University of the Arts.

Migration

At the beginning of the course, students and residents get to know each other and obtain a first impression of the problems of everyday life in Hall 9. Through further discussions, observations, and sketches, possible solutions are implemented as prototypes as quickly as possible and then discussed and tested in everyday use. Functional interventions and installations are thus created in cooperation with the residents.

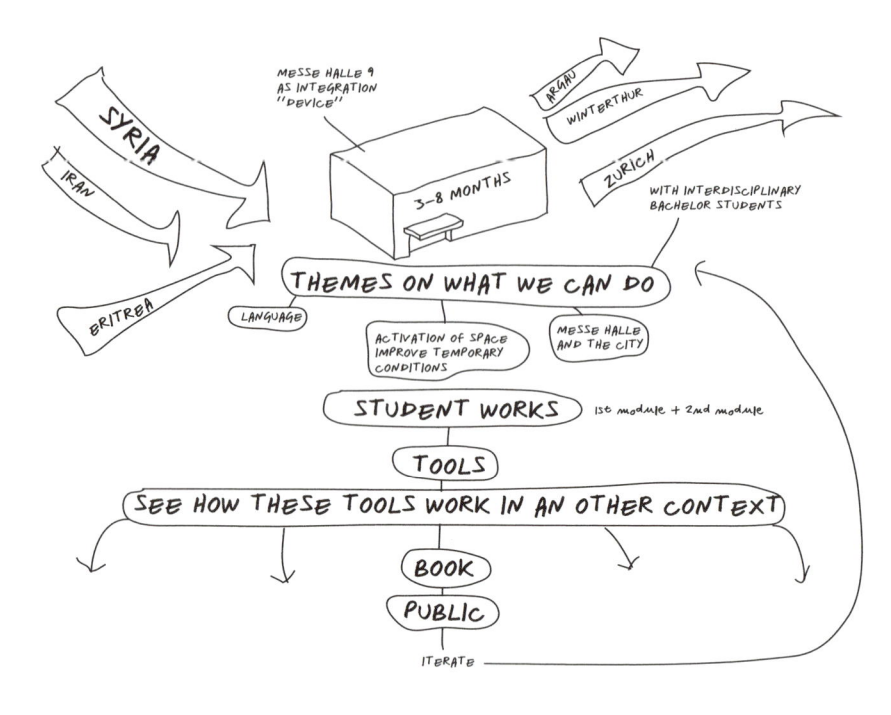

Migration

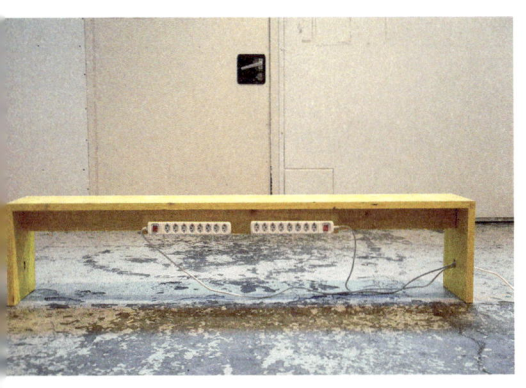

*mag*das Hotel
Caritas of the Archdiocese of Vienna,
AllesWirdGut Architekten, Daniel Büchel

Vienna, Austria
since 2015

The *mag*das Hotel is part of *mag*das Social Business, founded in 2012 by Caritas of the Archdiocese of Vienna. Based on the ideas of Muhammad Yunus, social issues should be solved in an entrepreneurial manner, whenever it is feasible and sensible.

In Austria, as elsewhere, people who have been forced to flee their home countries have difficulty finding work. This pilot project has created twenty jobs for recognized refugees from sixteen nations who work together with ten specialists from the hotel industry. At the same time, the project serves as a model for other endeavors, because it shows how refugees can be integrated into the labor market based on their abilities and talents.

The *mag*das Hotel was created by converting a former Caritas retirement home in collaboration with AllesWirdGut Architekten, the artist Daniel Büchel, and numerous volunteers. In view of the limited budget, reuse and upcycling were important aspects of the design concept—for example, the pre-existing built-in cabinets were converted into tables, lamps, and benches.

The economically self-sustaining *mag*das Hotel proves that an unusual concept can lead to a sustainable social project.

The conversion of the former Caritas retirement home was financed through a crowdfunding campaign and a five-year loan from Caritas. Donations in kind as well as furniture from Caritas's thrift store Carla completed the hotel and room furnishings.

Migration

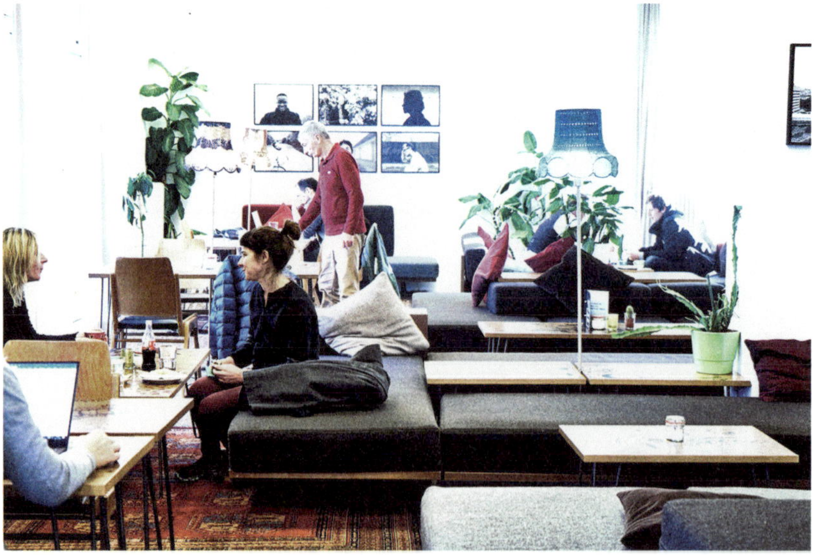

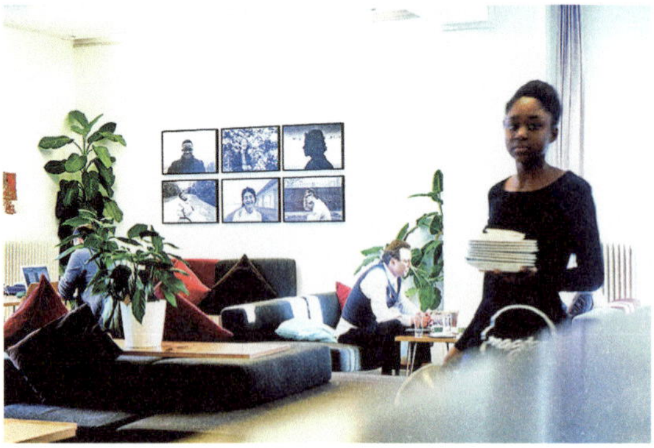

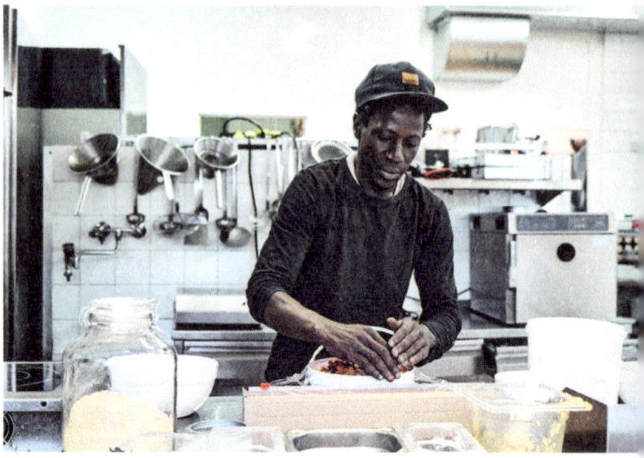

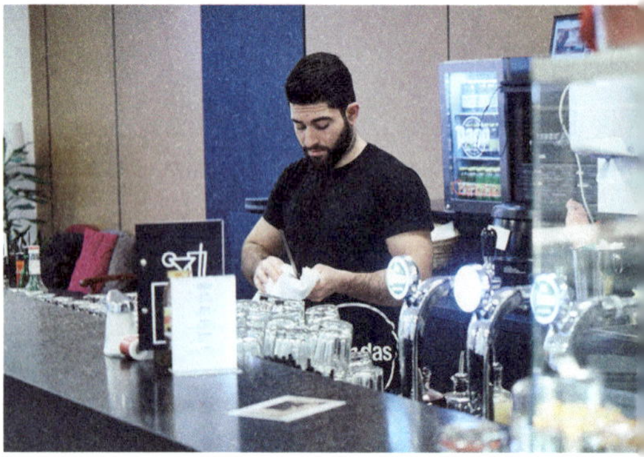

The hotel offers eighty-eight rooms in five categories. There is also the *mag*das Salon with a lounge, café, and bar, a library, a shop, the "Kunst im Hotel" project, a garden, and a boules area. The hotel and salon can be booked for events and seminars.

Migration

Social Design in Education and Research

Michael Krohn

Nearly forty years ago, Lucius Burckhardt noted that the design of a streetcar extends beyond the simple creation of the vehicle itself. A well-developed network, a tight timetable, affordable fares, and even clean cars: all of this is part of what can be called the streetcar design system. "Good design" therefore connects objects with social customs and standards.[1]

Design as an accomplishment of industrialization and an expression of "developed" societies creates many beautiful and practical things—and even though their use may be limited to a small portion of humanity, many people are impacted by the consequences.

When design students are confronted with the fact that design can also be understood to mean social construction in the sense that it serves as a catalyst for social change, this may not be new information, but it is surely still unusual. How can design methods open up a dialogue that improves social conditions? What does it mean to initiate inspiration, creativity, diversity, fresh perspectives, and the exchange of knowledge through a design-oriented approach?

Collaborative design processes with Macedonian textile makers

How can designers cooperate fruitfully with socially or economically focused organizations?

Project: Design with social impact

"Design with social impact" was a two-and-a-half-year joint teaching and research project initiated by the design department at Zurich University of the Arts.[2] Students, lecturers, researchers, and practice partners developed socially oriented design methods and concrete solutions for daily life within the scope of real projects. The goal was to gain insights into how to cooperate directly with the "people affected" in dealing with social and economic issues. Rather than seeking comprehensive solutions, the parties involved tried to develop and implement new procedures in collaboration with stakeholder groups, integrating ethnographic and exploratory methods, on-site work, human-centered design, and participatory design.

In recent years, several design projects with a focus on social impact have been initiated and successfully implemented. Design's capacity to shape not only objects but also relationships was still a new and compelling aspect for many of the participating students. The fundamental knowledge and standards of practice are still, however, incomplete. This project was mainly about demonstrating that design work done on-site together with those affected—often in socially and culturally unfamiliar contexts—can be very effective. The accompanying research provided a knowledge base and simultaneously served as the basis for setting up a "learning platform."

Students and craftswomen work on a reinterpretation of handcrafted Macedonian textiles.

Essential to this endeavor were the practice partners Swisscontact and Biovision Switzerland, which made local access possible and facilitated the integration of current projects from the field. They supported the project in many ways and at the same time provided critique. In addition, the undertaking was backed by a substantial contribution from the Stifung Mercator Schweiz.

"Design with social impact" included five workshops and summer courses with contexts that were specifically chosen for their diversity and their social relevance.[3] By way of illustration, two workshops are summarized here.

The Republic of Macedonia, currently a politically and economically unstable nation, finds itself in the situation of having many of its young emigrating directly after completing their education—a tragic "brain drain." In order for this situation to change, Swisscontact supports the development of small businesses specializing in fields such as handicrafts, tourism, agriculture, and food products. Students at Zurich University of the Arts and the Ss. Cyril and Methodius University in Skopje worked closely with local small and medium-sized businesses to not only bring their products and services to market but also to publicize them. In collaboration with a group of women who make traditional Macedonian knitwear, products were developed that are rooted in tradition but appeal to modern fashion sense. As this entailed a conflict between different aesthetic senses, the work required a great deal of sensitivity. All projects resulted in concrete prototypes or concepts. In addition to the design work, the project sought to provide local businesses with the tools and methods that would allow them to in turn develop their own ideas

Students learning basket weaving from Kenyan farmers

and concepts. The intensive cooperation culminated in an exhibition in Skopje. Only there did the authorities and the university realize the potential the local economy had if it could succeed in creating products and services, and ultimately jobs, using design methods.

In Kenya, Swiss, Kenyan, and Macedonian students spent three weeks working with small farmers who Biovision supports in their efforts in ecological agriculture. The students got to know the day-to-day life and problems of the farming families and subsequently analyzed work processes and products that, though traditional, have room for reconsideration. The families themselves were always included in this process—often giving rise to amazing feats of communication. The result was concrete solutions for the farmers that they could implement themselves with little effort. Making cultivation of the land more efficient or collaboratively coming up with a new concept for raising poultry may sound simple, but these things can have an enormous impact.

In Macedonia as well as in Kenya, the work required participants to analyze common patterns of thought and action and question why things are the way they are. Who has what interests? What limitations are there, what opportunities? Empathy, consideration, and understanding provide a foundation for people's empowerment, allowing them to actively participate and take ownership of the results, which also makes them more independent going forward. Social design has a double meaning here: designing social conditions and circumstances as well as designing artifacts and systems. Design as a discipline has an advantage in this sense, as it does not rely on a solid knowledge base but rather embeds operative and processual knowledge in an iterative procedure that places people at its center.

Workshop with Kenyan farmers and design students

Challenges and Opportunities

Although the conditions for the individual workshops were highly varied, the challenges were very similar: intensive intercultural and interdisciplinary cooperation, and the development and implementation of creative products and services and prototyping in a team, often under difficult circumstances (climate, resources, language, materials, etc.). But how can the quality of the results be measured? Can the usual design criteria be applied here? Yes and no. In participatory processes, designers relinquish control over the results and authorship in favor of collaboration, and to accept what is incomplete or in prototype form. They learn to handle limitations creatively and to cherish simple yet useful solutions, and this is a component of their success.

Understanding that design can trigger social change broadens the scope of the discipline and demonstrates how design can improve the quality of life and living conditions through creative processes. The solutions developed have a direct application in the daily life of those affected, and are simple, concrete, and pragmatic. Design thus becomes a partner of social institutions and organizations—and this is new. The aim here is not to make social workers or development aid workers out of young designers. Rather, they should be encouraged to make use of and expand the genuine knowledge and experience of the discipline. Moreover, social design can give the discipline a new dimension and significance in its practical and theoretical scope.

The workshops were guided and reflected upon by researchers. If social design is to have a real impact, a readily available base of knowledge, experience, and reflection must be developed and made accessible to other disciplines or partners. The research team's job was to synthesize and further develop the results, methods, and questions from the individual workshops in collaboration with the project partners. Their insights were published on a publicly accessible learning platform.[4] It is now up to the universities and practice partners to use, expand, and spread this knowledge.

1   Lucius Burckhardt, "Invisible Design" (1983), in *Design Is Invisible: Planning, Education, and Society,* Basel, 2017, pp. 27–35.
2   Project partners were: Ss. Cyril and Methodius University in Skopje, Macedonia; School of the Arts and Design, University of Nairobi, Kenya; School of Design, Jiangnan University, Wuxi, China; D&I Lab, Tongji University, Shanghai, China; Srishti Institute of Art, Design and Technology, Bangalore, India; National Institute of Design, Ahmedabad, India.
3   Winter 2016: "Planting Seeds of Design" in Zurich, Switzerland: Production, distribution and marketing of biological food products in Switzerland. http://dwsiswitzerland.tumblr.com/
Spring 2016: "Projects for Macedonia" in Skopje, Macedonia: Improvement of the employment situation in Macedonia in various economic sectors. http://dwsimacedonia.tumblr.com/
Summer 2016: "Frugal Design" in Zurich, Switzerland: Examining how better results can be achieved with limited resources. http://idss2016.tumblr.com/
Spring 2017: "Agriculture, Food and Consumerism" in Machakos, Kenya: Alternative food production, information, and distribution possibilities for small farmers in Kenya. https://dwsikenya.tumblr.com/
Summer 2017: "Elder and Younger" at Jiangnan University, Wuxi, China: What is the significance of the increasingly elderly populations of China, India, and Switzerland? https://idss2017.tumblr.com/
4   http://designwithsocialimpact.net/

Networks

The World Bank's *State of Electricity Access Report* (SEAR) states that 1.06 billion people, or 15 percent of the world's population, had to make do without electricity in 2017. Some 3.04 billion people still use solid fuels and kerosene for cooking and heating. Evidently, much still needs to be done to give everyone access to modern energy—one of the goals of the United Nations' 2030 Agenda for Sustainable Development.

    Energy supply is closely linked to other sustainable development goals such as health, education, food security, gender equality, poverty reduction, and combatting climate change. Innovative solutions secure the supply of energy and the availability of digital infrastructure while opening up development opportunities for individuals and the community. Solar energy plays a key role here.

Fairphone

Amsterdam, The Netherlands
since 2010

Based on a smartphone produced with as little exploitation of humans and nature as possible, the Dutch social business Fairphone is driving a movement for fair manufacturing of electronics in an effort to inspire those in the industry to do some rethinking. The company gives users more control over and responsibility for their phones, relying on long product life and simple repairs.

At the same time, Fairphone focuses on social values and works with manufacturers that offer safer and fairer working conditions. A central concern is to increase the transparency of supply chains in the electronics industry. The careful selection of raw materials plays a vital role here. The more than forty minerals and metals contained in a smartphone include some conflict resources such as tungsten, tin, tantalum, and gold, which are often mined under environmental, social, and political conditions that are cause for concern. Fairphone is involved in projects promoting conflict-free materials and recycling in order to reduce the amount of electronic waste generated. The mobile phone is still far from 100 percent fair, but the company is working step by step towards this goal.

Long-Lasting Design

Fair Materials

Good Working Conditions

Reuse and Recycling

Fairphone's strategy focuses on four core issues: phones that have a long service life and are easy to repair, the use of fair and conflict-free materials, safe and just working conditions, and product cycles that include reuse and recycling.

Tungsten mining in Rwanda: tungsten, which is required for the vibration mechanism in mobile phones, is later refined in Austria and transported to China for the production of the Fairphone 2.

Networks

The modular design of the phone makes
it easy to replace defective parts.

Fairphone supports and builds solutions to take back electronic waste from countries that lack formal and safe recycling structures, or funds new programs there like an e-waste recycling program in Ghana.

M-Pesa
Safaricom, Vodafone

Kenya
2007

M-Pesa is a mobile phone-based money transfer system that allows financial transactions to be carried out via a mobile phone. "M" stands for mobile, and "Pesa" means money in Swahili. The system, introduced in 2007 by the Kenyan telephone services provider Safaricom, a subsidiary of the British Vodafone Group, is now used by over two-thirds of all Kenyans. In areas with a weak infrastructure, the service can be used to make transfers via text message without needing to have a bank account, credit card, or internet connection. M-Pesa thus gives large parts of the Kenyan population the possibility of being paid for self-employment. There are no expensive fees, and transparent and traceable payment transactions help to reduce corruption and crime.

After a one-time registration with authorized M-Pesa agents—usually operators of gas stations, kiosks, or internet cafés—customers can make deposits to a virtual account or have cash paid out on-site. Once the M-Pesa menu is installed on a phone, purchases, electricity bills, and salaries can also be paid by text message. This successful model is now also being used in other countries.

The M-Pesa service is present in ten countries and serves more than 30 million active users.

Networks

M-Pesa is helping businesses to be more efficient. Businesses can pay for business transactions directly using the system, for example a wholesaler can distribute goods by truck and receive payments via M-Pesa from the retailers. In addition, businesses can receive payments from customers via the paybill facility and can also pay employees directly into their M-Pesa accounts.

Networks

One Laptop per Child

Miami, Florida, USA
since 2005

One Laptop per Child is a nonprofit organization created to provide children worldwide with a quality, innovative education. Basing its goals on the belief that learning is the foundation for human, social, and economic empowerment, OLPC creates educational opportunities for the world's poorest children by wanting to provide each child with access to a rugged, low-cost, connected laptop computer with content and software designed for collaborative, joyful, and self-empowered learning. The educational program is implemented to provide students with the opportunity to use technology in innovative and creative ways, to support and supplement existing curriculum, and to combat social exclusion.

OLPC was founded in 2005 by Nicholas Negroponte at the MIT Media Lab. Since then, the organization has delivered, in cooperation with governments, educational institutions, NGOs, and other donors, over 3 million XO laptops and tablets in twenty-five languages to sixty countries around the world. OLPC creates spaces for learning that involve families and the larger community. The one-to-one laptop program reduces the digital divide and is supporting the next generation of empowered, educated people.

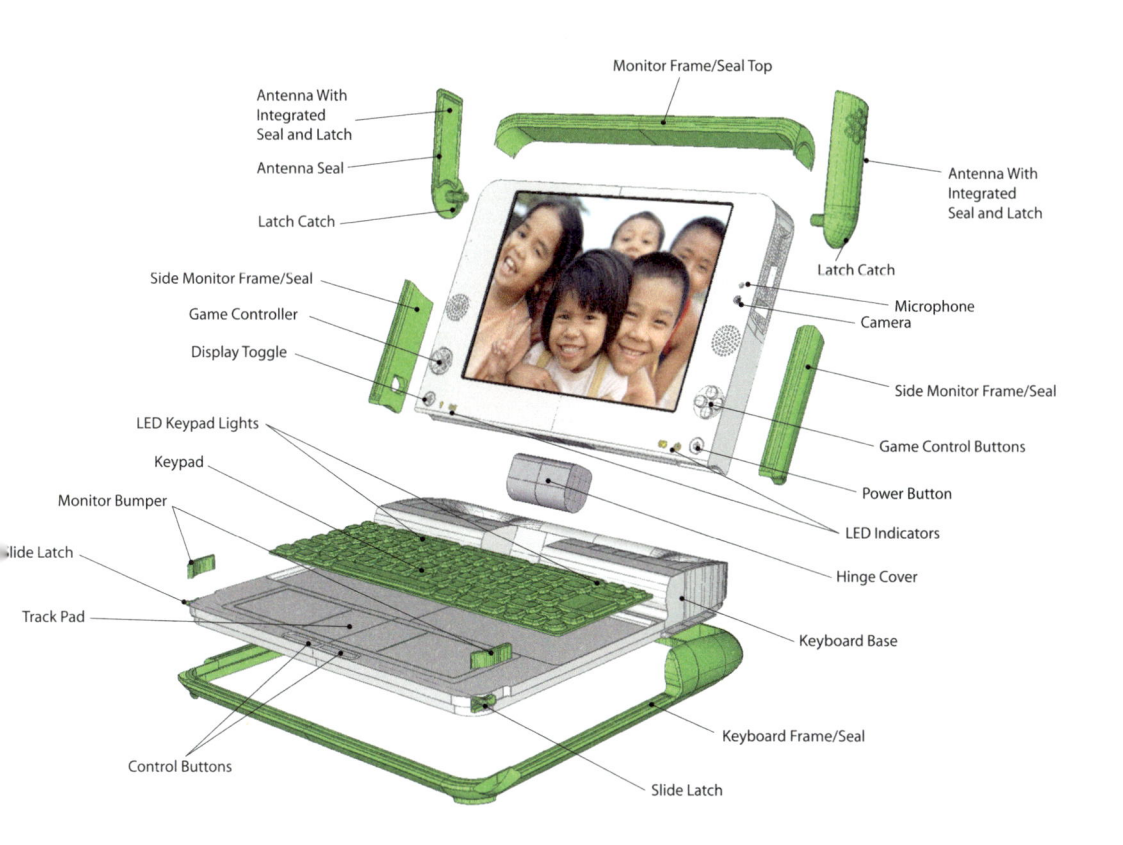

The XO Laptop is durable, functional, energy-efficient, and responsive. It was designed collaboratively by experts from academia and industry to combine innovations in technology and learning. Thanks to its flexible design and "transformer" hinge, the laptop easily assumes any of several configurations: standard laptop use, e-book reading, and gaming.

OLPC's learning strategy focuses on developing digital fluency. OLPC encourages students and teachers to think critically about learning and to reflect on the learning process. The OLPC program empowers children to create information and knowledge as they develop learning and innovation skills, including creativity, critical thinking, problem solving, and collaboration.

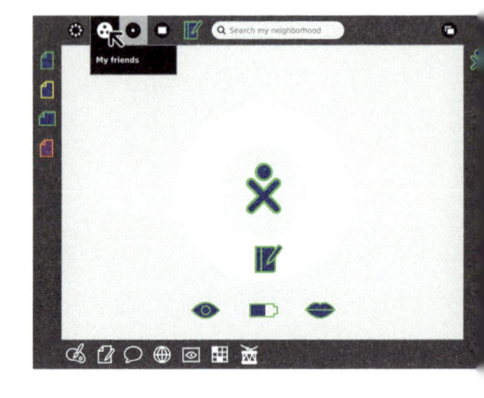

Networks

Solarkiosk
Graft / Lars Krückeberg, Wolfram Putz, Thomas Willemeit
with Andreas Spiess

Berlin, Germany
since 2009

The Solarkiosk is an energy-autonomous business cube that provides solar power, services, and products to rural and remote off-grid communities. Of the more than 1 billion people worldwide without electricity, 600 million live in Africa. These "off-grid households" spend on average 40 percent of their entire income on non-sustainable sources of power—a significant hazard for health and environment. In order to participate in the world's future development, they need a reliable, affordable, and clean source of energy.

Solarkiosk is an infrastructure instrument: the kiosk not only offers sustainable energy but is a service and communication center with last-mile distribution that creates an impact from the bottom up. The variety of services offered encompasses business, jobs, information, health, and entertainment. The integrated, self-sustaining, and secure system is a prefabricated, lightweight, robust, and easy-to-assemble "kit of parts" available in a variety of modular sizes. This social enterprise is currently expanding its business, providing power and space to refugee camps, health clinics, and schools.

With clean solar energy and an inclusive business model, Solarkiosk provides an energy supply, connectivity, and communication even in remote regions.

The basic model can be extended and modified to adapt to a wide variety of functions—depending on the local market. The unique expandability of the Solarkiosk E-Hubb frame can easily increase interior space and energy capacity. The E-Hubb can become the nucleus of a local mini-grid network as well as the village center.

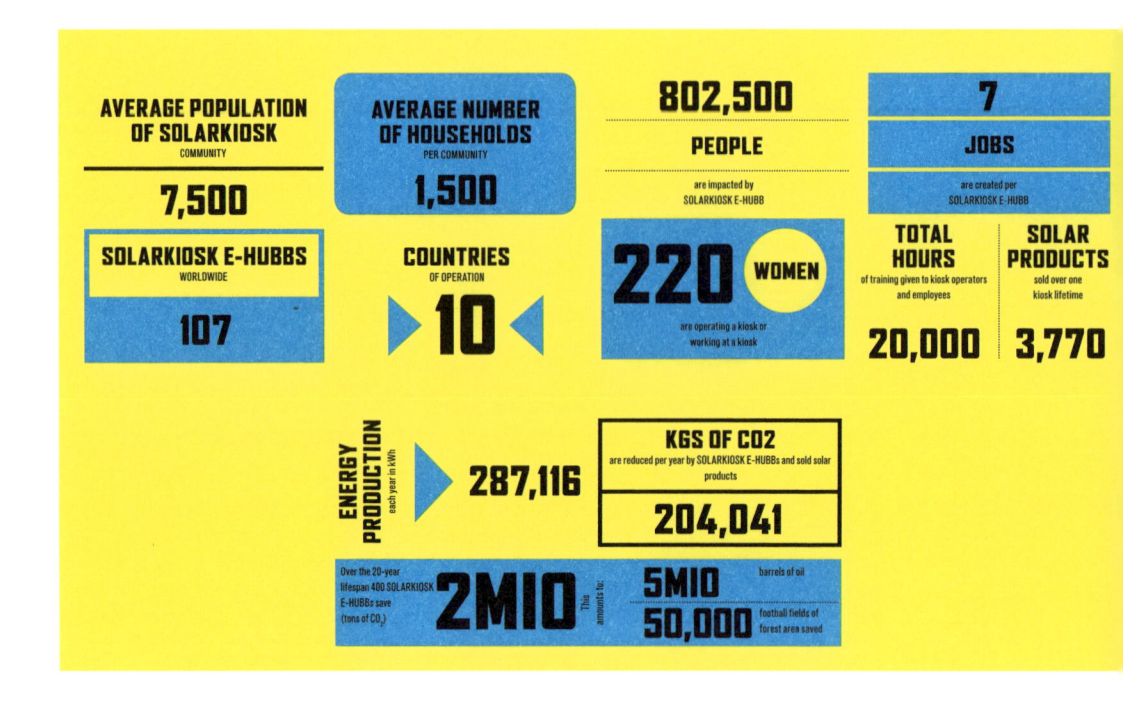

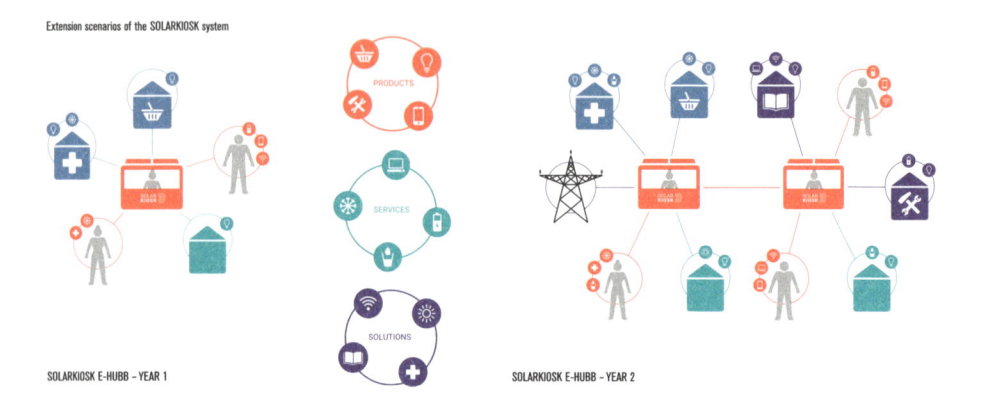

AVERAGE POPULATION OF SOLARKIOSK COMMUNITY
7,500

AVERAGE NUMBER OF HOUSEHOLDS PER COMMUNITY
1,500

802,500 PEOPLE are impacted by SOLARKIOSK E-HUBB

7 JOBS are created per SOLARKIOSK E-HUBB

SOLARKIOSK E-HUBBS WORLDWIDE
107

COUNTRIES OF OPERATION
10

220 WOMEN are operating a kiosk or working at a kiosk

TOTAL HOURS of training given to kiosk operators and employees
20,000

SOLAR PRODUCTS sold over one kiosk lifetime
3,770

ENERGY PRODUCTION each year in kWh
287,116

KGS OF CO2 are reduced per year by SOLARKIOSK E-HUBBs and sold solar products
204,041

Over the 20-year lifespan 400 SOLARKIOSK E-HUBBs save (tons of CO₂)
2 MIO

This amounts to:
5 MIO barrels of oil
50,000 football fields of forest area saved

Extension scenarios of the SOLARKIOSK system

SOLARKIOSK E-HUBB – YEAR 1

PRODUCTS
SERVICES
SOLUTIONS

SOLARKIOSK E-HUBB – YEAR 2

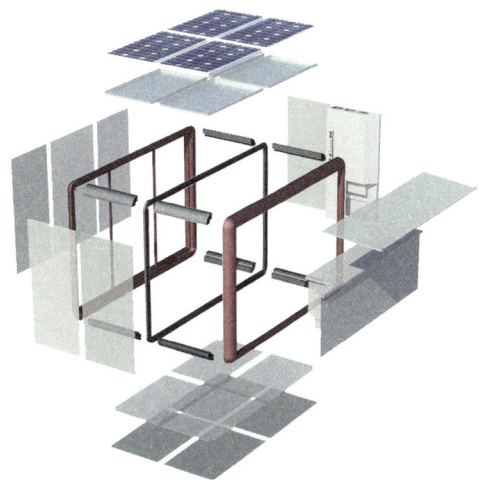

Solarkiosk E-Hubb is a kit of parts—extendable, flexible, modular—that is assembled on location. The individual packages of the kit are lightweight and thus transportable to rural, off-road areas.

Networks

The first Solarkiosks were implemented in Ethiopia. They offered mobile phone charging, cold drinks and a few selected solar products, always making sure that each kiosk was carefully embedded in and respected by the community. The success gave Solarkiosk the confidence to establish further kiosks, first in Kenya and Botswana, and then in Tanzania, Rwanda and Ghana.

Networks

Environment

Water scarcity, polluted water, and inadequate sanitation, hazardous light sources and cooking methods, the clearing of rainforests for palm oil and soy plantations, polluted soils, global warming with its predicted consequences such as the shifting of climate zones and rising sea levels, the decline in biodiversity, plastic waste in the oceans, the export of electrical waste, the political debate on the privatization of water sources and land grabbing—the list of environmental problems and their consequences is long.

Social design also means making proposals for a sustainable handling of the environment that allows people to live in dignity while respecting social and cultural contexts.

Little Sun
Olafur Eliasson, Frederik Ottesen

Berlin, Germany
since 2012

Little Sun is a social business and global project that brings clean, reliable, and affordable light to the more than 1 billion people in the world living in off-grid areas without electricity. Launched in London's Tate Modern in 2012, Little Sun is transforming lives through the power of sustainable energy and intelligent design.

By replacing unsafe and unhealthy kerosene lanterns with solar lamps, a family living off-grid can reduce their lighting costs by 90 percent over two years and receive stronger light. Charging Little Sun for a minimum of five hours in the sun produces four hours of bright light or up to fifty hours or more at the lowest level. This light can be used for cooking and eating, social encounters, studying, and work and trade.

Over 660,000 of the lamps were sold by the end of 2017. Every Little Sun sold at a higher price in areas of the world with electricity delivers one Little Sun to off-grid areas at a much lower, locally affordable price. The project empowers communities from the inside by creating local jobs and generating local profits through the local partners and a network of young, African entrepreneurs.

Artist Olafur Eliasson says, "Light is for everyone—it determines what we do and how we do it. This is why we have developed the solar-powered lamp Little Sun. One part of the artwork is the lamp and the activities it enables. The other is the successful distribution of Little Sun in off-grid communities, its journey from production to usage."

Environment

Little Sun is currently available in more than ten African countries, including Ethiopia, Senegal, South Africa, Rwanda, and Burkina Faso—as well as in Europe, Japan, Australia, Canada, and the United States. Little Sun uses on-grid investment to kickstart off-grid small businesses that sell Little Suns, providing funding for sales agents to receive business starter kits and micro-entrepreneurial training.

Environment

Warka Tower
Architecture and Vision / Arturo Vittori

Bomarzo, Italy
since 2015

Access to safe water should be a basic human right, but water poverty and conflicts over control of water resources continue to persist. Warka Water is an alternative water source for rural populations that face challenges in accessing drinkable water.

The water tower collects rain and harvests fog and dew, with the objective of providing an average of one hundred liters of drinking water per day. Built with simple tools and using a passive system to collect water from the atmosphere, Warka Water is designed to be owned and operated by the villagers. The canopy creates a shaded social space where the community can gather for public meetings. When a small rural community adopts Warka Water, it can lead to impactful change in a variety of areas, including the community's education, economy, society, and agriculture, as well as the environment.

After the installation of the first Warka Tower pilot in Ethiopia in early 2015, the Warka Water project is currently undertaking the first steps to bring the water tower to other places in Africa, Asia, and South America.

The name of the project Warka comes from the Warka tree, which is a giant, wild fig tree native to Ethiopia. Like the tree, the Warka Tower serves as an important cornerstone for the local community, becoming part of the local culture and ecosystem.

Environment

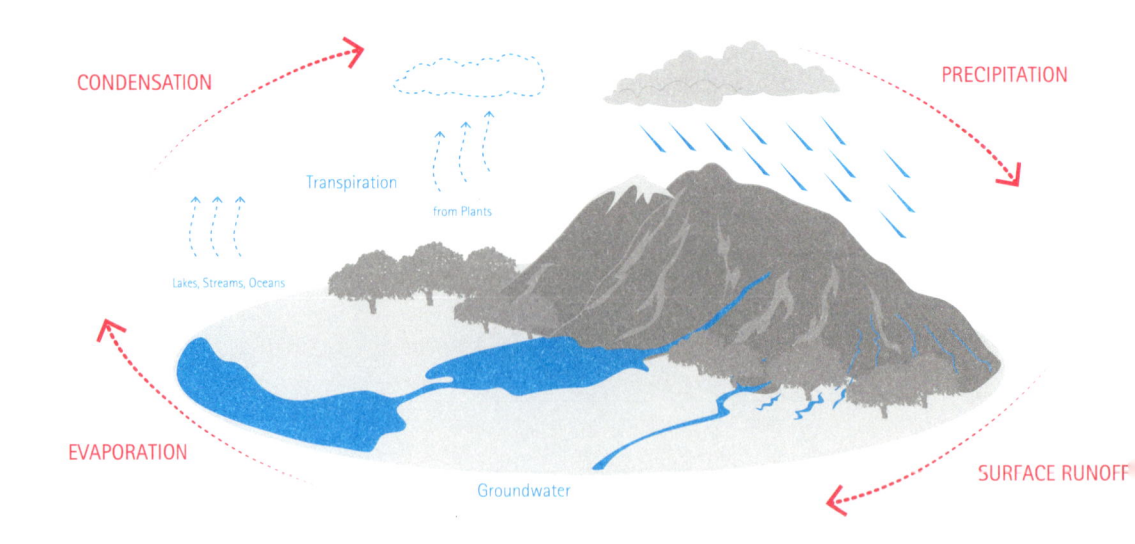

CONDENSATION PRECIPITATION

Transpiration
from Plants

Lakes, Streams, Oceans

EVAPORATION SURFACE RUNOFF

Groundwater

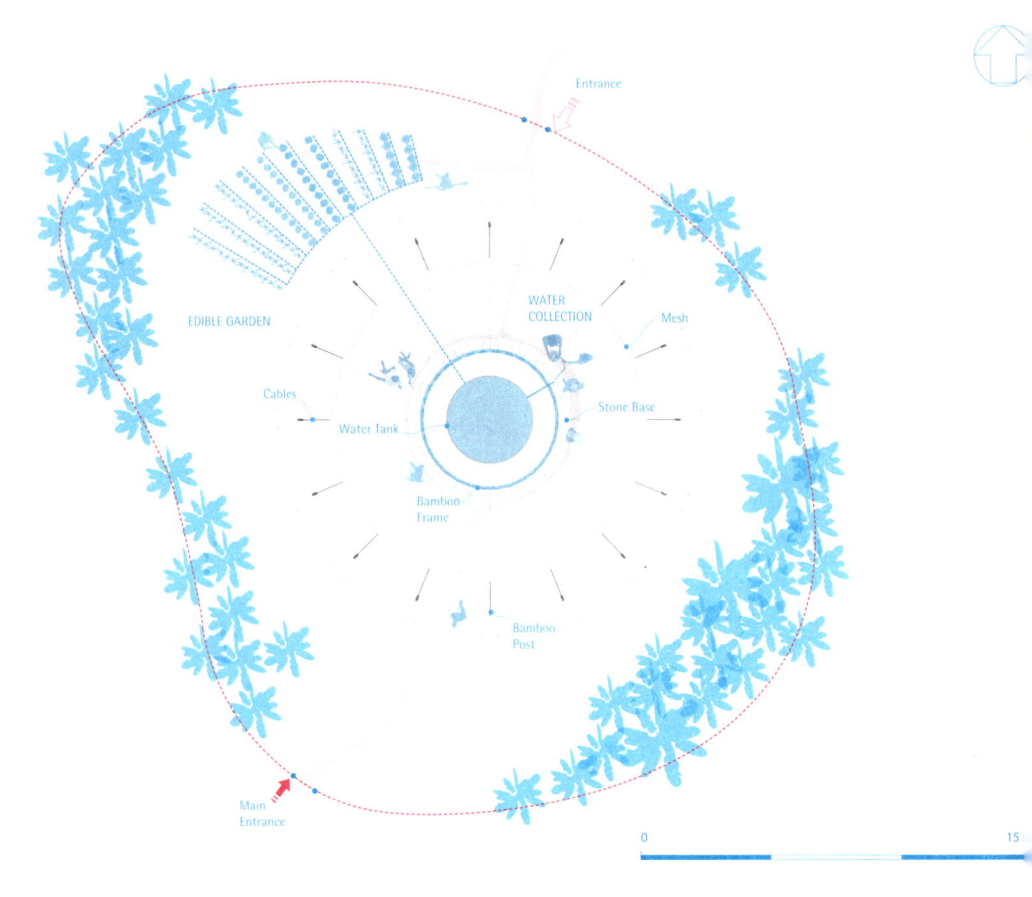

Entrance

EDIBLE GARDEN

WATER COLLECTION

Mesh

Cables

Water Tank Stone Base

Bamboo Frame

Bamboo Post

Main Entrance

0 15

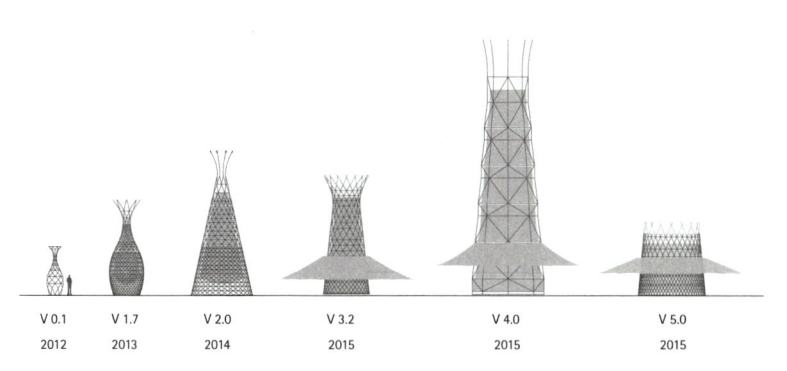

V 0.1	V 1.7	V 2.0	V 3.2	V 4.0	V 5.0
2012	2013	2014	2015	2015	2015

Air always contains a certain amount of water vapor, irrespective of local ambient temperatures and humidity conditions. This makes it possible to produce water from air almost anywhere in the world. Since 2012, Architecture and Vision has developed several design concepts and constructed twelve full-scale prototypes in order to test different materials within varying environmental conditions.

Environment

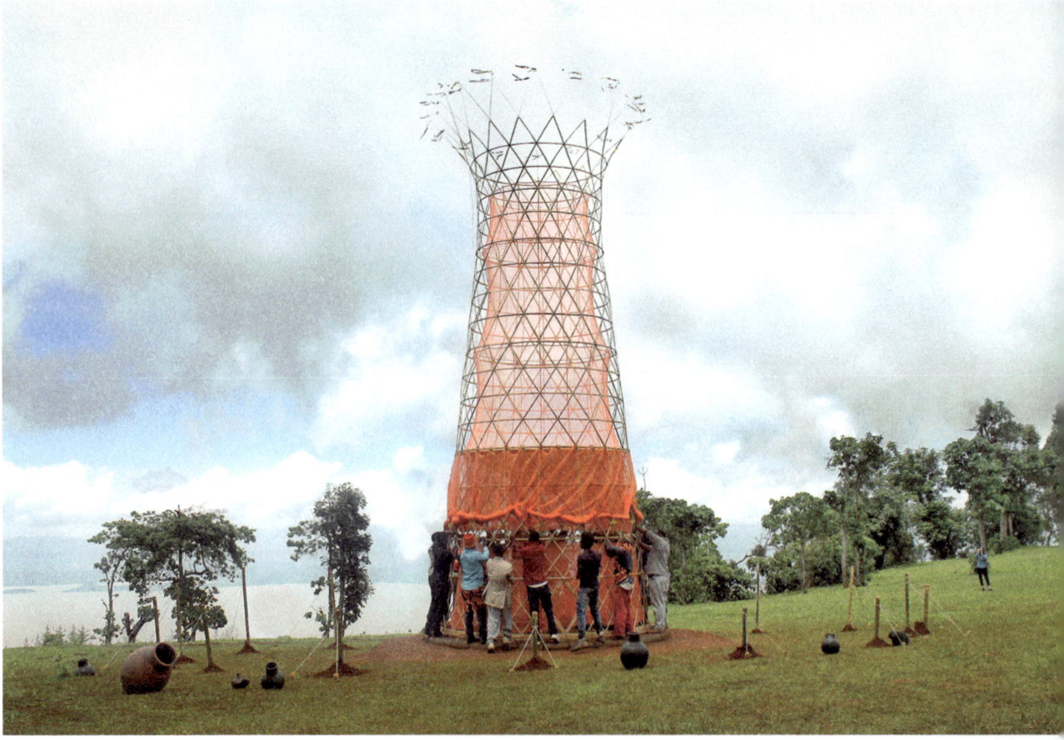

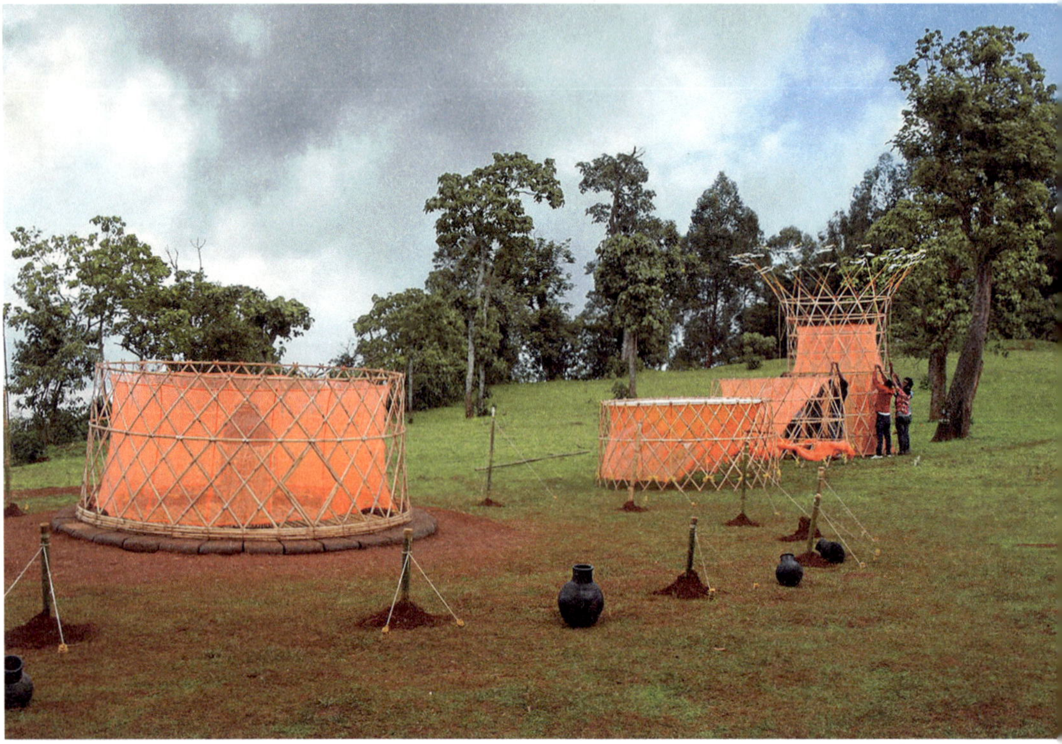

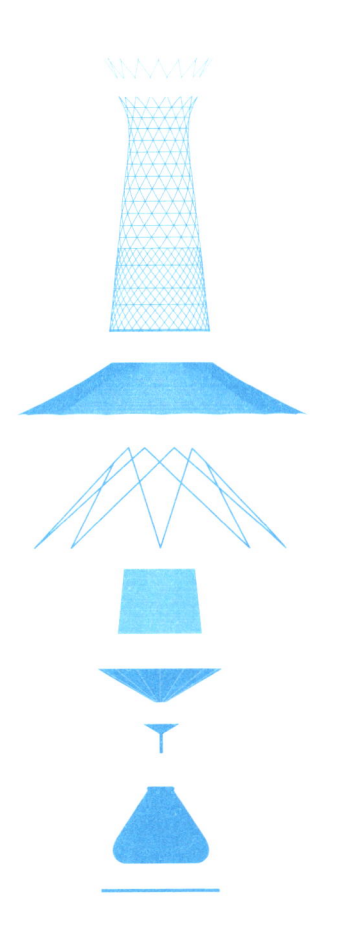

Warka Tower is realized with biodegradable and 100 percent recyclable materials. The philosophy of the project is to use local materials and traditional techniques as much as possible. The tower is also designed to be easily built with simple tools and maintained by local villagers without the need for scaffolding or electrical tools. The structure consists of six modules that are mounted together one after another from the bottom up.

Environment

Safir Water Filter
Zurich University of the Arts, Formpol AG, Eawag

Zurich, Switzerland
since 2010

In many regions of the world, access to clean water cannot be taken for granted. Insufficient or polluted water puts public health at risk. Boiling water to purify it only exacerbates the problem, as the use of common fuels such as wood or coal results in deforestation and erosion as well as massive CO_2 emissions.

The Safir water filter is able to purify heavily polluted water easily and efficiently. Environmental scientists and designers worked together closely in the development process, using an innovative method to create a product that is suitable for everyday use, can be inexpensively manufactured, and meets the cultural and functional requirements of its users. The principle is based on gravity flow and a biofilm, and thus no electricity or chemicals are needed. The service life is theoretically unlimited. The Safir filter is simply and robustly built from a double-walled container and offers a family their daily requirement of purified drinking water. The first prototypes were tested in Kenya in 2010, and the second prototype series was tested in 2013 with users in the Bolivian highlands. The water filter has been in series production since 2014.

Testing of the second prototype series in the Bolivian highlands: the design method is based on continuously adjusting and refining the water filter following the needs of the target group.

Environment

The individual parts of the Safir water filter are easy to manufacture and can be nested for transport. Only the production of the membrane module requires special expertise. Production, assembly, and distribution are possible on-site.

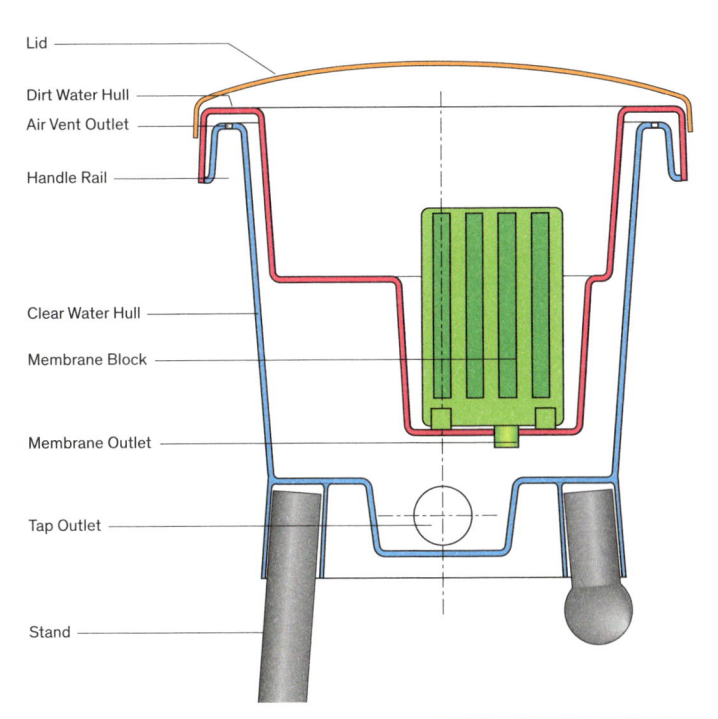

Lid
Dirt Water Hull
Air Vent Outlet
Handle Rail

Clear Water Hull
Membrane Block

Membrane Outlet

Tap Outlet

Stand

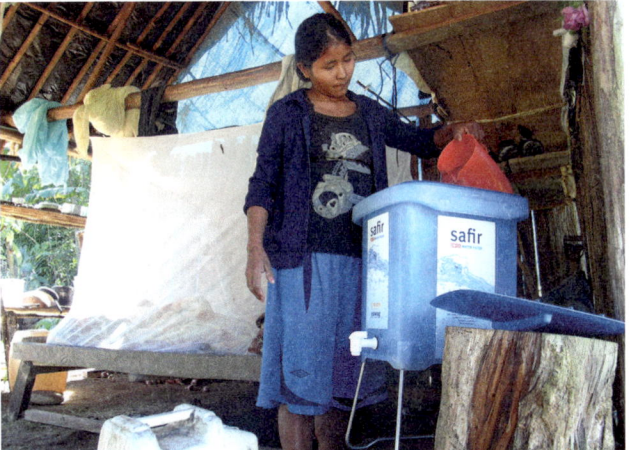

Environment 173

MoSan
Mona Chirie Mijthab

Zurich, Switzerland
since 2010

According to the World Health Organization, 2.5 billion people do not have access to safe and dignified sanitary facilities, posing a threat to both the environment and the health of the communities affected. Every day some 2,000 children worldwide die of diarrhea due to this situation.

After a stay in Bangladesh, Mona Mijthab began developing the MoSan sanitation solution. The portable dry toilet, which separates urine from feces, provides hygiene and privacy for families in developing countries. Furthermore, excrement is made use of here as a valuable resource. The sanitation system was developed through co-creation in a participatory design process and also includes educational work in the communities, a collection service, and a recycling process. The excrement is processed into fertilizer or fuel, which is then resold to create economic added value for the community.

The system, which has been tested and further developed in pilot studies with users in Kenya, ensures more humane living conditions, protects the environment and water sources, and creates jobs in the region. This holistic solution is currently being implemented with Mayan communities in Guatemala.

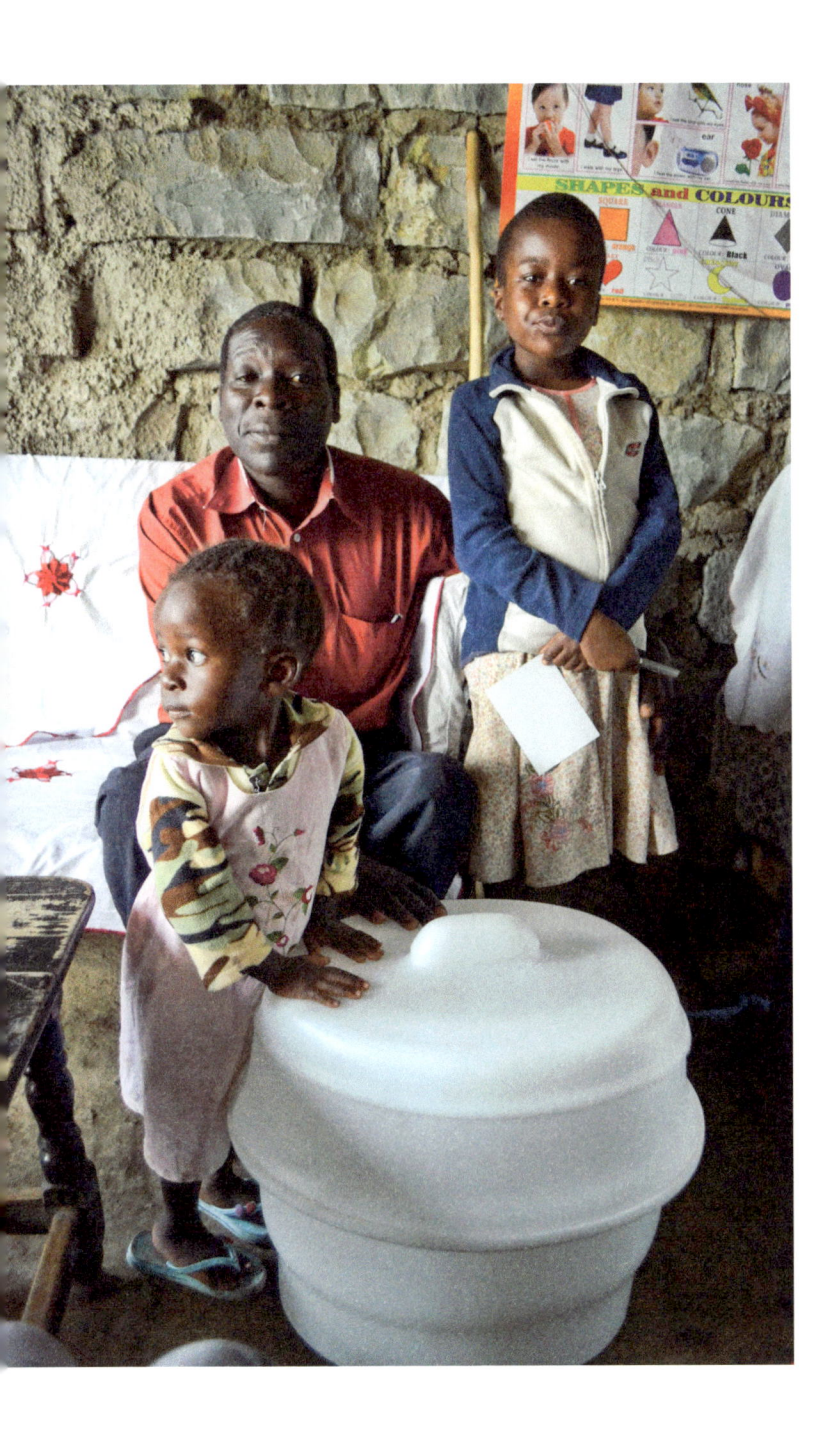

Cooperation with families in Naivasha, Kenya, to test and refine the system and service concept for the MoSan dry toilet (2013–15). For the users, having their own toilet is a status symbol.

Environment

The system not only improves hygiene and safety but also creates job opportunities where it is deployed, and improves economic conditions. The recycling of feces provides natural fertilizers or fuels that can replace chemical products and firewood and thus mitigate climate change. In the future, MoSan will function as a franchise that can be implemented worldwide.

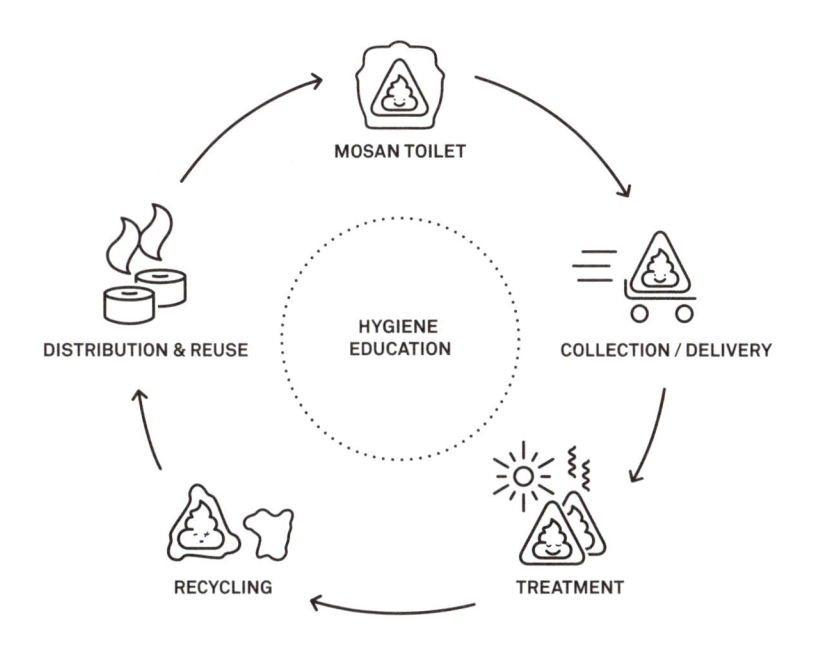

MOSAN TOILET

COLLECTION / DELIVERY

TREATMENT

RECYCLING

DISTRIBUTION & REUSE

HYGIENE EDUCATION

Environment

177

10,000 Gardens for Africa
Slow Food Foundation for Biodiversity, Terra Madre

since 2010

Slow Food, a grassroots movement active in 160 countries, is based on the principle that everyone has a right to good food, as well as a responsibility to society, culture, agriculture, and sustainability. One of their projects is the creation of 10,000 gardens in Africa. Since 2010, more than 3,000 gardens have been planted at schools, in villages, and on the outskirts of cities in thirty-five African countries. Slow Food thus seeks to promote agriculture based on knowledge of the terrain and respect for biodiversity and local cultures. This concept recognizes the dignity, history, and knowledge of African communities and ensures their food supply without threatening social relations or destroying the environment.
    Slow Food gardens grow traditional, robust varieties of fruit, vegetables, and aromatic and medicinal herbs that have adapted to local conditions over the course of centuries. The gardens are practical models of sustainable agriculture and are easy to reproduce. They could very well point the way to an alternative course of development in Africa in which food production is linked to local communities and environmental preservation.

Watering a garden in Burkina Faso: water resources are used sparingly. Rainwater is collected and soil moisture is protected by mulching and drip irrigation.

SLOW FOOD GARDENS IN AFRICA

- 🧑‍🌾 **3072** GARDENS IN AFRICA
- 🧑‍🌾 **356** NEW GARDENS IN 2017-2018
- 🌍 **35** COUNTRIES
- 🌍 **29** FORMATIONS IN 2018
- 🧍 **80,000** PEOPLE INVOLVED
- 🧍 **50** AGRONOMISTS INVOLVED

Map values:
30, 67, 36, 46, 19, 60, 154, 49, 100, 91, 95, 19, 154, 106, 96, 115, 46, 20, 8, 309, 423, 143, 200, 147, 49, 15, 116, 128, 3, 10, 3, 11, 47, 153, 4

Slow Food works to make people more aware of the wealth of resources on the African continent and its extraordinary biodiversity: communities, people, and their knowledge are at the heart of all projects.

Environment

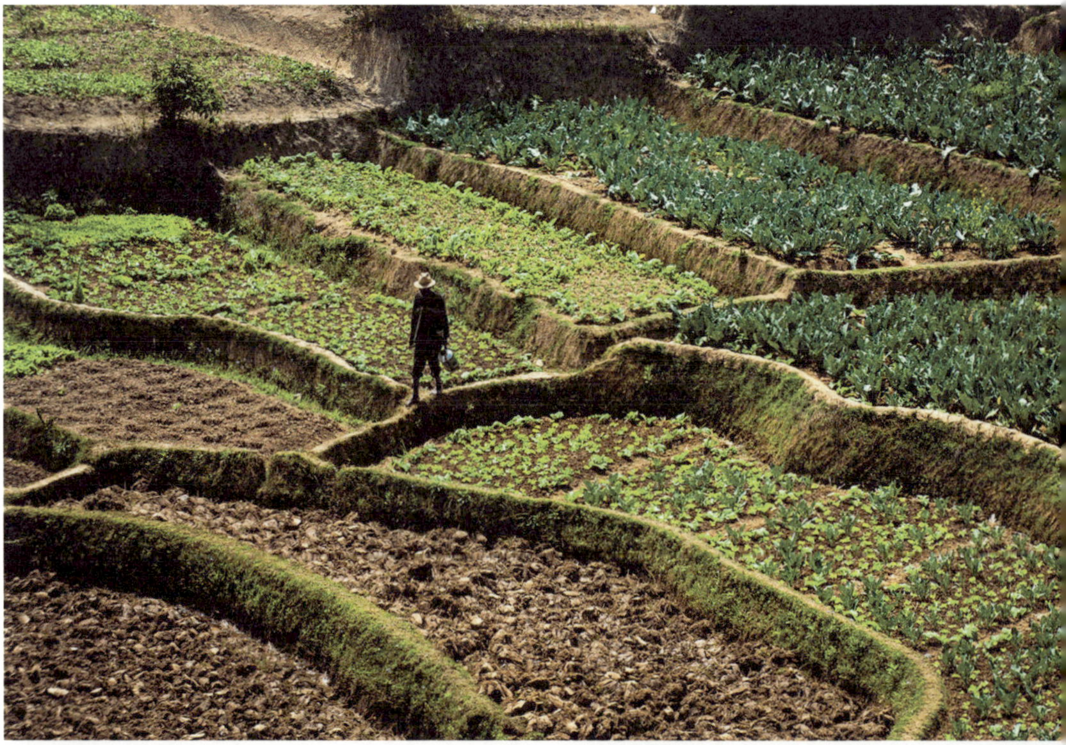

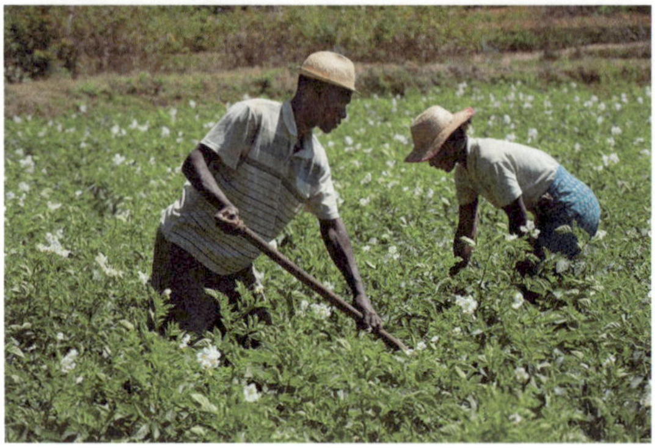

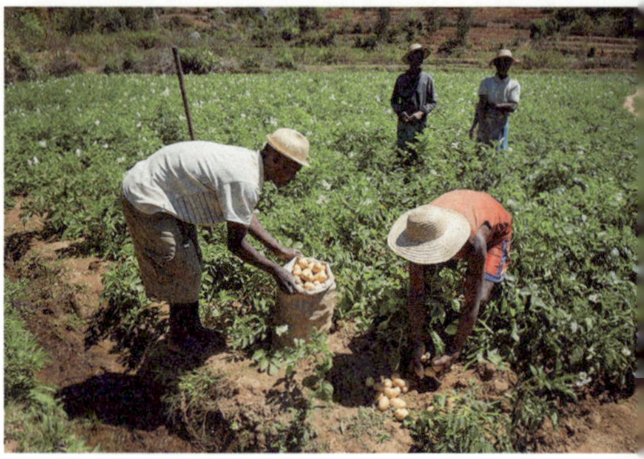

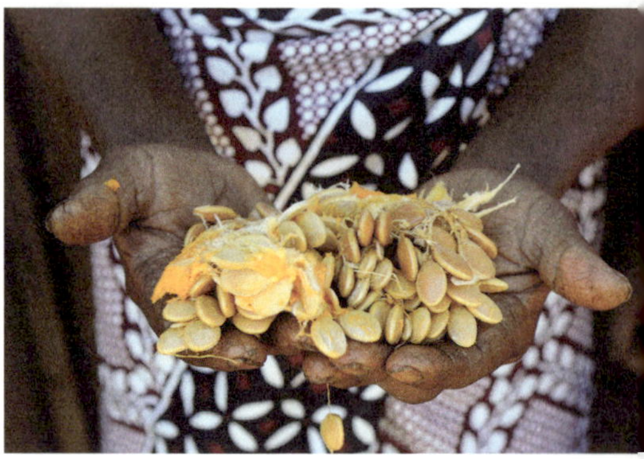

Participants in the program produce their own seeds in seed beds and use composted plant waste, manure, and ash as fertilizers while avoiding the use of pesticides.

Environment

Authors

Claudia Banz

Claudia Banz, a curator and art historian, has been design curator at the Kunstgewerbemuseum Berlin since 2017. From 2011 to 2017 she headed the Department of Art and Design at the Museum für Kunst und Gewerbe Hamburg, where she was responsible for redesigning the permanent exhibit on *Art Nouveau and Modernism* as well as the Department of Design.

In parallel, she curated the special exhibitions *Fast Fashion: The Dark Side of Fashion, Art Nouveau: The Great Utopian Vision,* and *Food Revolution 5.0: Design for Tomorrow's Society.* In 2014, she organized the conference "Social Design: History, Practice, Perspectives."

Banz had previously worked as a freelance curator for numerous international exhibitions, including *Africa Remix: Contemporary Art of a Continent* (Museum Kunstpalast, Düsseldorf), *Glück. Welches Glück* (Deutsches Hygiene-Museum, Dresden), *Dressed! Art en Vogue* (Museum Kunstpalast, Düsseldorf), *Triumph of the Blue Swords: Meissen Porcelain for Aristocracy and Bourgeoisie* (Staatliche Kunstsammlungen Dresden), and *Unresolved Matters: Social Utopias Revisited* (Utrecht Manifest, Biennial for Social Design 2009).

She has published texts on twentieth- and twenty-first-century art, design, and fashion, and has served as editor of publications including *Dressed! Art en Vogue* (*Kunstforum International* 197, 2009), and *Social Design* (*Kunstforum International* 207, 2011). Her book *Social Design. Gestalten für die Transformation der Gesellschaft* was published in 2016, and the exhibition catalogue *Food Revolution 5.0* came out in 2017.

Michael Krohn

Michael Krohn is head of the Master of Arts in Design program and deputy director of the Design Department at the Zurich University of the Arts (ZHdK).

With a background in industrial design and design engineering, his academic interests have invariably been propelled by research, education, and innovation. Combining experiences from design practice with his academic development has led to different positions at the ZHdK since 1992. After developing the Media Lab, conducting various research projects, and later as head of the Industrial Design program, he was part of the reorganization of the Design Department to better cope with future design challenges focusing on scientific, social, and technological aspects rather than on arts and crafts. Parallel to that, since 2000 he has been running his own design agency FORMPOL.

He has written and published on a wide range of scientific and popular topics. As a member of the CUMULUS Executive Board II and III, he initiated the International Design Summer School, conducted each year in Switzerland, China, and India, as well as regular collaborations with institutions of higher education worldwide.

Angeli Sachs

Studied art history, German, and sociology at the universities of Augsburg and Frankfurt am Main. She is currently a professor and the head of the Master of Arts in Art Education Curatorial Studies program at Zurich University of the Arts (ZHdK) and curator at the Museum für Gestaltung Zürich.

Prior to this she was head of the Master of Arts in Art Education program at ZHdK (2014–17), head of exhibitions at the Museum für Gestaltung Zürich (2006–12), editor in chief for architecture and design at Prestel Verlag in Munich (2001–05), academic assistant at the Institute for History and Theory of Architecture, Swiss Federal Institute of Technology in Zurich (1995–2000), realized freelance academic work for the Deutsches Architekturmuseum in Frankfurt am Main (1994–95), and was press officer for the Frankfurter Kunstverein (1990–93).

She has curated numerous exhibitions and contributed to and edited publications on architecture, design, art, and culture of the twentieth and twenty-first centuries. For the Museum für Gestaltung Zürich: *Design Studio: Processes,* 2017; *Do It Yourself Design* (with Franziska Mühlbacher and MAK Vienna), 2015; *Out to Sea? The Plastic Garbage Project* (with Christian Brändle), 2012 (traveling exhibition); *Black and White—Designing Opposites,* 2011; *Global Design,* 2010; *Nature Design,* 2007; and for other institutions: *Jewish Identity in Contemporary Architecture* (with Edward van Voolen, Joods Historisch Museum, Amsterdam et al.), 2004; and *Museums for a New Millennium* (with Vittorio Magnago Lampugnani, Hessenhuis, Antwerp et al.), 1999.

Her most recent publication is *Contemporary Curating and Museum Education* (co-edited with Carmen Mörsch and Thomas Sieber), Bielefeld, 2017.

Bibliography

General

Claudia Banz, ed., *Social Design, Kunstforum International* 207 (March–April 2011).

Claudia Banz, ed., *Social Design. Gestalten für die Transformation der Gesellschaft,* Bielefeld, 2016.

Friedrich von Borries, *Weltentwerfen. Eine politische Designtheorie,* Berlin, 2016.

Amanda Breytenbach and Kathryn Pope, eds., *Design with the Other 90%: Changing the World by Design,* Conference Proceedings, Cumulus Johannesburg, September 22–24, 2014, Johannesburg, 2014.

Max Bruinsma and Ida van Zijl, eds., *Design for the Good Society: Utrecht Manifest 2005–2015,* Rotterdam, 2015.

Lucius Burckhardt, *Design Is Invisible: Planning, Education, Society,* Basel, 2012.

Lucius Burckhardt, *Writings: Rethinking Man-made Environments,* ed. Jesko Fezer and Martin Schmitz, trans. Jill Denton, Vienna and New York, 2004.

Benedict Clouette and Marlisa Wise, *Forms of Aid: Architecture of Humanitarian Space,* Basel, 2017.

Design for the Other 90%, ed. Cynthia E. Smith, exh. cat. Smithsonian Cooper-Hewitt, National Design Museum, New York, 2007.

Anthony Dunne and Fiona Raby, *Speculative Everything: Design, Fiction, and Social Dreaming,* Cambridge, MA and London, 2013.

Davide Fassi, Anna Meroni, and Giulia Simeone, "Design for Social Innovation as a Form of Design Activism: An Action Format" (2013), www.desisnetwork.org/2018/02/17/design-for-social-innovation-as-a-form-of-design-activism-an-action-format.

Global Design: International Perspectives and Individual Concepts, ed. Angeli Sachs, exh. cat. Museum für Gestaltung Zürich, Baden, 2010.

Internationales Design Zentrum Berlin, ed., *Design? Umwelt wird in Frage gestellt,* Berlin 1970.

Wolfgang Jonas, Sarah Zerwas, and Kristof von Anshelm, eds., *Transformation Design: Perspectives on a New Design Attitude,* Basel, 2016.

Lucy Kimbell, "Designing Future Practices," unpublished notes for a talk held at the symposium Making/Crafting/Designing, Akademie Schloss Solitude, Stuttgart, 2011, http://www.lucykimbell.com/stuff/Kimbell_MakingCrafting_Feb2011_public.pdf.

Ezio Manzini, *Design, When Everybody Designs: An Introduction to Design for Social Innovation,* Cambridge, MA and London, 2015.

Bruce Mau and Institute without Boundaries, *Massive Change,* London and New York, 2004.

Yana Milev, *Designsoziologie. Der erweiterte Designbegriff im Entwurfsfeld der Politischen Theorie und Soziologie,* Frankfurt am Main, 2014.

Stephan Moebius and Sophia Prinz, eds., *Das Design der Gesellschaft. Zur Kultursoziologie des Designs,* Bielefeld, 2012.

Nature Design: From Inspiration to Innovation, ed. Angeli Sachs, exh. cat. Museum für Gestaltung Zürich, Baden, 2007.

Victor Papanek, *Design for the Real World: Human Ecology and Social Change,* London, 1984; 2nd rev. ed. 2011.

Reporting from the Front, ed. Alejandro Aravena, Biennale Architettura 2016, 2 vols., Venice, 2016.

Richard Sennett, *Together: The Rituals, Pleasures and Politics of Cooperation,* New Haven and London, 2012.

Bernd Sommer and Harald Welzer, *Transformationsdesign. Wege in eine zukunftsfähige Moderne,* Munich, 2014.

Karl Stocker, ed., *Socio-Design. Relevante Projekte: Entworfen für die Gesellschaft / Relevant Projects: Designed for Society,* Basel, 2017.

Marjanne van Helvert, ed., *The Responsible Object: A History of Design Ideology for the Future,* Amsterdam, 2016.

Nigel Whiteley, *Design For Society,* London, 1993.

Muhammad Yunus, *Creating a World Without Poverty: Social Business and the Future of Capitalism,* New York and London, 2008.

Muhammad Yunus, *Building Social Business: The New Kind of Capitalism that Serves Humanity's Most Pressing Needs,* New York, 2010.

Urban Space and Landscape

Assemble: How We Build / Wie wir bauen, ed. Angelika Fitz and Katharina Ritter, exh. cat. Architekturzentrum Wien, Zurich, 2017.

Ricky Burdett and Deyan Sudjic, eds., *The Endless City: The Urban Age Project by the London School of Economics and Deutsche Bank's Alfred Herrhausen Society,* London and New York, 2007.

Ricky Burdett and Deyan Sudjic, eds., *Living in the Endless City: The Urban Age Project by the London School of Economics and Deutsche Bank's Alfred Herrhausen Society,* London and New York, 2011.

Anton Falkeis and Lukas Feireiss, eds., *Social Design—Public Action: Arts as Urban Innovation,* Vienna and Basel, 2015.

Jan Gehl, *Cities for People,* Washington, DC, 2010.

Maria Nicanor et al., *100 Urban Trends: A Glossary of Ideas from the BMW Guggenheim Lab,* Solomon R. Guggenheim Foundation, 3 editions, New York, 2013; Berlin, 2013; Mumbai, 2013, http://www.bmwguggenheimlab.org/100urbantrends.

Marcos L. Rosa and Ute E. Weiland, eds., *Handmade Urbanism: From Community Initiatives to Participatory Models,* Berlin, 2013.

Antonio Scarponi, *ELIOOO – How to Go to IKEA® and Build a Device to Grow Food in Your Apartment,* Zurich, 2013.

Richard Sennett, *Building and Dwelling: Ethics for the City,* London, 2018.

Housing, Education, Work

Genossenschaft Kalkbreite, *Kalkbreite. Ein neues Stück Stadt,* Zurich, 2015.

Andres Lepik, ed., *Francis Kéré: Radically Simple,* Ostfildern, 2016.

Si/No: The Architecture of Urban-Think Tank (*Slum lab No. 10*), Munich, 2016.

Hilde Strobl, Natalie Schaller, and Heike Skok, *Keine Angst vor Partizipation! Das kleine ABC des gemeinsamen Bauens und Wohnens / Don't Be Afraid to Participate The Little ABC of Communal Planning and Housing,* ed. Architekturmuseum der TU München, Mitbauzentrale München, Ostfildern, 2016.

Together! The New Architecture of the Collective, ed. Mateo Kries et al., exh. cat. Vitra Design Museum, Weil am Rhein, 2017.

Urban-Think Tank, *Unsolicited Architecture,* Ostfildern, 2018.

Production

Fast Fashion. Die Schattenseiten der Mode, ed. Sabine Schulze and Claudia Banz, exh. cat. Museum für Kunst und Gewerbe Hamburg, 2015.

Elke Gaugele, ed., *Aesthetic Politics in Fashion,* Berlin, 2014.

Enzo Mari, *Autoprogettazione?,* Mantova, 2002; 6th ed. 2015.

Migration

Shigeru Ban, *Humanitarian Architecture,* exh. cat. Aspen Art Museum, New York, 2014.

Shigeru Ban and Keio University SFC Ban Laboratory, *Voluntary Architects' Network: Making Architecture, Nurturing People: From Rwanda to Haiti,* Tokyo, 2010.

Peter Cachola Schmal, Oliver Elser, and Anna Scheuermann, eds., *Making Heimat: Germany, Arrival Country,* German Pavilion at the 15th International Architecture Exhibition– La Biennale di Venezia 2016, Ostfildern, 2016.

Networks

Graft, Lars Krückeberg, Wolfram Putz, and Thomas Willemeit, *Architecture Activism,* Basel, 2016.

Environment

Food Revolution 5.0. Gestaltung für die Gesellschaft von morgen, ed. Claudia Banz and Sabine Schulze, exh. cat. Museum für Kunst und Gewerbe Hamburg, Dortmund, 2017.

Slow Food, *Bite Size, Slow Food: Save Biodiversity, Save the Planet* (brochure), Carrù, 2015, http://slowfood.com/filemanager/Whatwedo/INGexpo.pdf.

Image Credits

8/9: Zhang Peng / LightRocket / Getty Images
10/11: ROBERTO SCHMIDT / AFP / Getty Images
12/13: KEYSTONE / AP Photo / Mandel Ngan
14/15: KEYSTONE / AP Photo / A.M. Ahad
16/17: Thomas Trutschel / Photothek / Getty Images
18/19: KEYSTONE / DPA / Roberto Pera
20: Bauhaus-Archiv Berlin / Lyonel Feininger, Titelblatt des Bauhaus-Manifestes, 1919, © 2018, ProLitteris, Zurich
22: © Victoria and Albert Museum, London
25: © Kramer Archiv, photography: Grethe Leistikow, 1929
26: Adriano Alecchi / Mondadori Portfolio / Getty Images
27: © Stadtarchiv Kassel, E 1 N 7000 Eichen, Renate Lehning
33–35: Antonio Scarponi / Conceptual Devices, Zürich
37–43: GEHL / ENERGY FOUNDATION
45–47: Foodmet Brussels, © ORG Permanent Modernity, photography: © Filip Dujardin
49–54: Images courtesy of Assemble
55 top, center: Images courtesy of Granby Workshop and Assemble, photography: Rob Battersby
55 bottom: Images courtesy of Granby Workshop and Assemble
59: Photography: Christian Brunner, Zürich
60 top: Genossenschaft Kalkbreite, Pasquale Talerico
60 center: Genossenschaft Kalkbreite, Res Keller [translated by the publisher]
60 bottom: Genossenschaft Kalkbreite
61–63: Photography: Volker Schopp
65, 66 top, 67 top, 68 bottom: © raumlaborberlin
66 bottom: © Stefanie Zofia Schulz
67 bottom: © Sebastian Latz / raumlaborberlin
68 top, 69: © Fred Moseley / S27
68 center: © Stephanie Steinkopf, Ostkreuz / S27
71–73, 75 bottom left: © Robust Architecture Workshop, photography: Kolitha Perera
74, 75 top, bottom right: Angeli Sachs
77/78: © ETHZ U-TT / Daniel Schwartz
79: © ETHZ U-TT
80/81: © ETHZ U-TT / David Southwood
83, 86, 87 top: Photography: Iwan Baan
84/85, 87 bottom: © Kéré Architecture
99–101: © Ateliers Chalamala, photography: Jonas Marguet, Vevey
103–5: © Andreas Möller
107, 109 top: © Cucula, photography: Verena Bruening
108 top: © Cucula
108 center, bottom: © Cucula, photography: Fred Moseley
109 center, bottom: © Cucula, photography: Jonas Holthaus
113–17: © Shigeru Ban Architects
119: Photography: One Young World
120: Photography: Angela Luna
121 top: David Rogers / Getty Images Sport / Getty Images
121 center, bottom: Photography: Asteroide Films
123, 124 bottom, 125: © ZHdK
124 top: © ZHdK, Antonio Scarponi
127–29: © Peter Barci / magdas
130/131: © ZHdK, photography: Mona Altheimer
132/133: © ZHdK, photography: Ivana Chaloska
139–42, 143 bottom: © Fairphone
143 top: © Fairphone, photography: Joost de Kluijver
145, 146 top, bottom left, 147 center, bottom: © Vodafone
146 bottom right, 147 top: Photography: Philip Mostert
149, 150 top, bottom, 151 bottom: © OLPC, Inc.
150 center: © OLPC, Inc. / Sugar Labs
151 top: © OLPC, photography: Mathilde Mahoudeau
153, 156: Andreas Spiess, SOLARKIOSK AG
154 top: GRAFT / proxi.me
154 down, 155 center, bottom: SOLARKIOSK AG
155 top: GRAFT
157 top: Georg Schaumberger
157 bottom: SIMON MULUMBA / CMONCY IMAGES

Acknowledgments

161, 162 bottom: Studio Olafur Eliasson
162 top: Little Sun
163 top: Michael Tsegaye
163 bottom: Helen Zeru
165–69: © Warka Water Architecture and Vision
171/172, 173 center, bottom: © ZHdK, photography: Selina Derksen-Müller, EAWAG
173 top: © ZHdK, FORMPOL AG
175–77: © Mosan
179: © Serena Milano
180: © Slow Food
181 top, 182 top: © Paola Viesi, Madagascar
181 bottom: © Paola Viesi, Sierra Leone
182 center: © Paola Viesi, South Africa
182 bottom: © Oliver Migliore, Kenya
183: © Paola Viesi, Sierra Leone and Mozambique

Cover: Solarkiosk, Botswana, photography: Andreas Spiess, SOLARKIOSK AG. Lycée Schorge Secondary School, Burkina Faso, axonometric view of the project: © Kéré Architecture

Every effort has been made to locate all copyright holders. Should we have been unsuccessful in individual cases, copyright claims should be addressed to the Museum für Gestaltung Zürich.

We would like to thank all participating architects, designers, craftspeople, photographers, institutions, and organizations for their cooperation and assistance with the project.

Museum für Gestaltung Zürich

SOCIAL DESIGN
Participation and Empowerment

An exhibition and publication of the Museum für Gestaltung Zürich
Christian Brändle, Director

Curator: Angeli Sachs

Publication
Concept and texts: Angeli Sachs
Project management and editing: Petra Schmid, Angeli Sachs
Assistance and image research: Léonie Süess
Translation (Ger.–Eng.): Jennifer Taylor
Copyediting: Jonathan Fox
Proofreading: Stephanie Shellabear
Design: Integral Lars Müller / Lars Müller and Alice Poma
Production: Martina Mullis
Lithography: prints professional, Berlin, Germany
Printing and binding: DZA Druckerei zu Altenburg, Germany
Paper: Munken Lynx, 130 g/m^2
Typeface: Theinhardt Regular

© 2018
Zürcher Hochschule der Künste, Zürcher Fachhochschule
Lars Müller Publishers

Z hdk
Zürcher Hochschule der Künste
Zurich University of the Arts

Museum für Gestaltung Zürich
Ausstellungsstrasse 60
P.O. Box
CH-8031 Zurich
museum-gestaltung.ch / eMuseum.ch

Lars Müller Publishers
Pfingstweidstrasse 6
CH-8005 Zurich
lars-mueller-publishers.com

Distributed in North America by ARTBOOK | D.A.P.
www.artbook.com

ISBN 978-3-03778-570-6
First edition

Printed in Germany